AF480870

BIOTECH HORIZON:- EXPLORING THE FRONTIERS OF INNOVATION

DR. RAJESH JORGEWAD

Made with ♥ on the Notion Press Platform
www.notionpress.com

This book is dedicated to the beloved parents of the student authors and also to their Professors for their utmost support, and never ending inspiration throughout the study. They are the ones who have provided the resources that were needed in the preparation of this book. It is also dedicated all the teachers who were behind the student auhors to make this research possible by guiding the authors to complete the study.

Also, this book is dedicated to the Kolhapur Institute of Technology's College of Engineering (Autonomous), Kolhapur for giving an opportunity to the researchers to nurture, test their skills, and cooperation to build this study.

Last but not the least, we look up and dedicate this book/study to our Almighty God who has given us the strength, knowledge, wisdom, protection, and will continue and keep positive to finish this study.

Contents

Contents

Foreword

In "Biotech Horizon: Exploring the Frontiers of Innovation," we embark on a journey through the captivating landscape of biotechnology, guided by the expertise of four visionary authors. In a world where the boundaries between science fiction and reality blur with each passing day, this book serves as a compass, navigating the uncharted territories of biotech innovation.

As our understanding of life sciences expands, so too does our ability to harness the power of biology for the betterment of humanity. From groundbreaking discoveries in genetic engineering to revolutionary advancements in healthcare, the potential of biotechnology knows no bounds. However, with great power comes great responsibility, and the authors of this book deftly navigate the ethical and societal implications of our newfound capabilities.

Through meticulous research, insightful analysis, and compelling storytelling, "Biotech Horizon" offers readers a glimpse into the future of medicine, agriculture, energy, and beyond. Whether you are a seasoned scientist, a curious enthusiast, or simply a citizen of the world, the knowledge contained within these pages is sure to inspire, provoke thought, and ignite the imagination.

Join us on this exhilarating expedition as we venture beyond the horizon of possibility, exploring the frontiers of innovation that will shape the future of our planet and redefine what it means to be human.

Preface

In "Biotech Horizons: Exploring the Frontiers of Innovation," readers embark on a journey through the captivating realm of biotechnology which is at the forefront of both societal change and scientific advancement. This book offers a comprehensive investigation of biotechnology's enormous potential through its 12 carefully constructed chapters, which explore the field's many applications, ramifications, and future prospects. This book serves as a comprehensive guide to the myriad applications, implications, and future prospects of biotechnological innovation, as humanity stands on the cusp of unprecedented scientific and technological advancement.

Through its 12 meticulously crafted chapters, readers are provided with a panoramic view of the field, from its foundational principles to its most cutting-edge developments. The applied science of using living organisms and their by-products for commercial development is known as biotechnology, and it has grown and evolved to such an extent in recent years that an increasing number of professionals work in fields directly impacted by the science. This book presents the most recent information and developments from this field. This book provides experts and students across a wide range of the life sciences, including genetics, immunology, biochemistry, agronomy, and animal science, with an engaging and colourful overview of biotechnology for the first time.

A lay reader without a background in science who wants an engaging and educational introduction to the main ideas in biotechnology will also find this book interesting. The book covers every important facet of the field, including environmental biotechnology, transgenic animals, analytical biotechnology, viruses, antibodies, and vaccines, as well as food biotechnology, enzymes, genetic engineering, and the human genome. The easiest way to get a thorough introduction of this complicated area is with this engaging book.

Acknowledgements

We would like to thank our Head Of the Department Dr. Pallavi Patil and our supervisor Dr. Rajesh Jorgewad for the valuable advice and support they have given us throughout our research and in writing this book. We would also like to thank them for their guidance and encouragement. We are also very thankful to the librarian and staff of Central and Departmental Library of KITCOEK for their support and help in providing us with the essential references. We acknowledge with thanks the support and dedication rendered by all our team members.

Co-Authors:
1. ABHISHEK SHIVAJI MOHITE
2. ADITYA MANOJ PILLAI
3. DHANWANTARI DHANANJAY DESAI

Prologue

This book includes 12 chapters. They are:

1. Breaking Grounds: An Introduction to Biotechnology.

2. Unlocking Nature's Blueprint: The Power of Genetic Engineering.

3. Revolutionizing Medicine: The Rise of Biopharmaceuticals.

4. Industrial Biotechnology: Transforming Processes, Products and Perspectives.

5. Harvesting Innovations: Agricultural Biotechnology.

6. Engineering Life: Exploring Synthetic Biology.

7. Decoding Life: Exploring Bioinformatics.

8. Nature's Engineers: Environmental Biotechnology for a Sustainable Future.

9. Nano-Horizons: Exploring Biotechnology at the Nano-scale.

10. Frontiers Beyond Earth : Biotechnology in Space Exploration.

11. BioRevolution: Navigating Challenges and Seizing Opportunities in Biotechnology.

12. Horizon's Unveiled: Emerging Trends and Future Directions in Biotechnology

Key Features Of The Book

KEY FEATURES:-

Provides content that is understandable to readers who lack a strong foundation in science.

Includes all facets of biotechnology applications.

Contains a summary, annotated references, links to useful websites, at the end of each chapter.

Presents more than 50 colour figures.

Written in an enthusiastic and engaging style unlike other existing theoretical and dry-style biotechnology books

A Note To The Readers From The Authors

DEAR READERS,

"Welcome to "Biotech Horizon," where the realms of science fiction intersect with the breathtaking possibilities of biotechnology. In this compelling journey, you'll discover a captivating exploration of the cutting-edge advancements reshaping our world and challenging the very fabric of what it means to be human. From genetic engineering to synthetic biology, this book unveils the thrilling potential and ethical dilemmas of our biotechnological future. Prepare to embark on a thought-provoking odyssey that will redefine your understanding of life itself."

"Embark on a journey into the heart of tomorrow with "Biotech Horizon." In these pages, you'll uncover the astonishing frontiers of biotechnology, where science fiction meets reality. Delve into the depths of genetic manipulation, bioengineering, and the blurred lines between natural and artificial. Whether you're a seasoned scientist, a curious thinker, or simply intrigued by the future, this book promises to ignite your imagination and provoke profound questions about the world we inhabit and the one we're shaping. Join us as we peer over the horizon into a brave new era of possibilities."

"Dive into the realms of regenerative medicine, genetic modification, and bio-inspired technologies as we unravel the mysteries of life itself. Whether you're a visionary entrepreneur, an inquisitive scholar, or an avid reader with a thirst for knowledge, this book promises a riveting journey into the future of humanity. Prepare to be captivated, enlightened, and forever changed by the wonders that lie beyond the horizon."

CHAPTER ONE

BREAKING GROUNDS: AN INTRODUCTION TO BIOTECHNOLOGY

INTRODUCTION:

In order to create technologies and goods that enhance both our quality of life and the environment, the multidisciplinary area of biotechnology applies concepts from biology, chemistry, physics, and engineering. Fundamentally, biotechnology uses the innate abilities of living things or their cellular constituents to produce useful goods and procedures. This can include changing organisms, tampering with genetic material, or using biological systems for a variety of purposes.

Biotechnology is a broad field that covers many important subjects likes:

1. Healthcare:

The development of vaccinations, medications, and diagnostic instruments is made possible by biotechnology, which is a key factor in the field of medicine. The manufacturing of biopharmaceuticals and genetic engineering have transformed the way diseases are treated by providing possibilities for personalised medicine and targeted therapy.

2. Agriculture:

The application of biotechnology in agriculture results in higher crop yields, better nutritional value, and enhanced resilience to pests and diseases. Biotechnological techniques were used to create genetically modified (GM) crops, which have advantages including lower pesticide use and more sustainable agricultural methods.

3. Industrial Biotechnology:

Biotechnology stimulates innovation in industrial processes, making it easier to produce biofuels, bioplastics, and biochemicals from renewable resources. This is known as industrial biotechnology. Enzymes and microorganisms are used in biocatalysis, which produces useful compounds, and bioremediation, which removes pollutants from the environment.

4. Environmental Protection:

Biotechnology can help with pollution control, trash management, and conservation initiatives, among other environmental problems. Microorganisms are employed in bioremediation techniques to break down toxic pollutants, and biofuels made from renewable resources contribute to a decrease in greenhouse gas emissions and a reduction in the need for fossil fuels.

5. Research and Development:

Biotechnology serves as the foundation for scientific investigations in a wide range of fields by offering instruments and approaches for examining biological systems, comprehending the causes of illness, and creating novel technologies. Proteomics, bioinformatics, and genomics are among the fields that provide thorough examination of biological data, leading to breakthroughs and discoveries.

6.Bioremediation:

Bioremediation is the practice of cleaning contaminated environments by using live organisms or their metabolic processes. To eliminate contaminants from soil, water, and air, biotechnological methods improve the microbial degradation processes that occur naturally. Bioremediation techniques use microorganisms that can degrade harmful substances like pesticides, heavy metals, and hydrocarbons to reduce pollution in the environment and rebuild ecosystems.

7. Pharmaceuticals and biologics:

The creation, discovery, and manufacturing of pharmaceutical medications and biologics are greatly aided by biotechnology. Genetically modified organisms or cell lines can be used to synthesise therapeutic proteins, antibodies, and vaccinations thanks to recombinant DNA technology. Biopharmaceuticals, which are sourced from biological sources, provide more effective and safe targeted treatments for a range of ailments, such as cancer, infectious diseases, and autoimmune disorders.

8. Biodefense & Biosecurity:

Biotechnology plays a part in efforts to protect national security and public health from biological threats through biodefense and biosecurity. Rapid identification, characterisation, and reaction to infectious diseases, bioterrorism agents, and developing pandemics are made possible by sophisticated biotechnology techniques. Vaccines, diagnostics, antiviral medications, and biosurveillance systems are all part of biodefense techniques, which are designed to reduce the threat of biological weapons and natural disasters.

9. Energy:

The development of sustainable energy production methods and renewable energy sources is aided by biotechnology. Enzymatic or fermentation techniques are used to convert biomass into biofuels like ethanol and biodiesel. Developments in biotechnology also facilitate the synthesis of materials and chemicals obtained from biomass as substitutes for goods derived from fossil fuels. Furthermore, the utilisation of microbial fuel cells and biogas technologies allows for the production of power from organic waste materials by utilising the metabolic activities of microorganisms.

10. Consumer Products:

Biotechnology is present in common consumer goods like textiles, household cleansers, cosmetics, and personal hygiene items. Renewable resource-based biobased substances provide environmentally friendly substitutes for petroleum-based chemicals, lessening their impact on the environment and improving the sustainability of the final product. Innovations in biotechnology also aid in the creation of bio-based materials for a variety of uses, including biodegradable polymers, biofibers, and biomaterials.

Historical Review:

1. Ancient Biotechnology Practices:

Investigate prehistoric biotechnological methods used by humans, such as fermentation for the creation of beverages and food preservation.

Emphasise how microbial processes were used by ancient societies for baking, brewing, and dairy fermentation, which laid the groundwork for contemporary biotechnological developments.

2. The Advent of Contemporary Biotechnology:

Talk about important findings in biology and microbiology, such as Louis Pasteur's formulation of the germ theory and Robert Hooke's discovery of cells, that served as the foundation for contemporary biotechnology.

Honour the efforts of researchers such as Friedrich Miescher, who discovered nucleic acids, and Gregor Mendel, who developed the laws of heredity.

3. Recombinant DNA Technology:

Follow the evolution of recombinant DNA technology throughout the 20th century, starting with Werner Arber, Daniel Nathans, and Hamilton Smith's discovery of restriction enzymes.

Describe the groundbreaking studies carried out in the 1970s by Stanley Cohen and Herbert Boyer, which proved that genetic material could be transferred between various creatures and paved the way for the development of genetic engineering.

4. Biotechnology Benchmarks:

Highlight significant turning points in the history of biotechnology, such as Cohen and Boyer's 1973 development of Escherichia coli, the first organism to be genetically altered using a foreign gene.

Talk about how Kary Mullis invented the polymerase chain reaction (PCR) in 1983, which transformed molecular biology research and DNA amplification.

5. The Human Genome Project:

Describe the global scientific endeavour to map and sequence the entire human genome that was started in 1990.Talk about how the Human Genome Project has advanced our knowledge of human health, genetics, and genomics, as well as the implications it has for genetic research and personalised medicine.

6. Applications of Biotechnology In Medicine:

Examine how biotechnology is being used in healthcare and medicine, including the creation of gene treatments, monoclonal antibodies, and recombinant protein therapeutics.

Highlight innovations include the creation of biopharmaceuticals to treat conditions like cancer and autoimmune disorders and the use of recombinant DNA technology to produce insulin.

7. Agricultural Biotechnology:

Talk about the introduction of genetically modified (GM) crops with improved characteristics like pest resistance, herbicide tolerance, and increased nutritional value.

Examine the arguments and controversies surrounding genetically modified crops, taking into account worries about socioeconomic issues, the environment, and food safety.

8. Industrial Biotechnology

It has developed and how it is being used to produce biofuels, biochemicals, and biopolymers from renewable resources.Emphasise the developments in biocatalysis, fermentation technology, and metabolic engineering that have increased the variety of bio-based goods and environmentally friendly production methods.

9. Ethical And Regulatory Challenges:

The ethical and regulatory challenges posed by biotechnological breakthroughs should be addressed. These include worries about genetic privacy, biopiracy, and equal access to biotechnologies.Talk about the legal frameworks that control biotechnology research, development, and commercialization. You should also talk about the need for well-balanced laws that uphold moral and safety standards while encouraging innovation.

10. Prospects For The Future:

Discuss potential future paths and cutting-edge biotechnology developments, such as personalised medicine, synthetic biology, and genome editing based on CRISPR.Examine how biotechnology can be used to solve urgent global issues including food security, infectious illnesses, and climate change, as well as how it will affect how humans and the environment develop in the future.

Fundamental Principles In Biotechnology:

1. Cell Theory And Genetics:

Explain the cell theory, which holds that all living things are made of cells, and talk about its importance in biotechnology in relation to genetics. Describe the fundamental concepts of genetics that underpin biotechnological research and applications, such as genetic diversity, gene expression, and inheritance.

2. Central Dogma of Molecular Biology:

Explain the Central Dogma of Molecular Biology, which describes how genetic information moves from DNA to RNA to proteins. Describe how this principle controls biotechnological processes like gene cloning and protein expression, which are essential to biotechnological procedures like transcription, translation, and protein synthesis.

3. DNA Structure And Function:

Discover the structure of DNA, including the double helix, the makeup of nucleotides, and complementary base pairing. Talk about how genetic information is carried by DNA and how biotechnological procedures like DNA sequencing and gene editing affect it.

4. Recombinant DNA Technology:

This refers to the technique of fusing DNA molecules from many sources to produce unique genetic sequences. Describe the steps involved in recombinant DNA technology, including DNA ligation, transformation, and restriction enzyme digestion, which allow for the modification and cloning of genes.

5. Gene Expression And Regulation:

Discuss transcription, RNA processing, translation, and other aspects of gene expression, as well as how these processes are regulated in response to environmental and cellular inputs. Examine the regulation of gene expression by transcription factors, enhancers, and promoters. Discuss the implications for biotechnological applications such as synthetic biology and gene therapy.

6. Structure And Function of Proteins:

Explain the primary, secondary, tertiary, and quaternary structures of proteins as well as their functions.

Draw attention to the various functions that proteins play in biological processes including signal transmission, enzymatic catalysis, and structural support. You should also discuss the significance of proteins in biotechnological applications such protein therapies and enzyme engineering.

7. Enzymology And Biocatalysis:

Describe the fundamentals of enzymology, such as substrate selectivity, cofactor requirements, and enzyme kinetics. Talk about the engineering of enzymes for increased activity and stability as well as their uses as biocatalysts in industrial processes like bioremediation, the synthesis of biofuels, and pharmaceutical manufacture.

8. Microbiological Technology:

Examine the various applications of microorganisms in biotechnology, such as bioprocessing, bioremediation, and fermentation. Talk about the fundamentals of genetics, physiology, and metabolism of microorganisms as well as how bacteria can be genetically engineered for uses in synthetic biology and metabolic engineering.

9. Cell Culture And Bioprocessing:

Explain the fundamentals of cell culture, including in vitro cell growth, maintenance, and differentiation. See also Cell Culture and Bioprocessing. Talk about the uses of cell culture techniques in biotechnology, including the synthesis of monoclonal antibodies, recombinant proteins, and cell-based medicines. You should also touch on the difficulties and factors to be taken into account when extending bioprocesses for industrial production.

10. Computational Biology And Bioinformatics:

Describe the fundamentals of computational biology and bioinformatics, covering systems biology techniques, structure prediction, and sequence analysis. Talk about how bioinformatics databases and tools are used to analyse biological data, forecast gene function, and create new biotechnological solutions. You should also talk about how computational approaches are combined with experimental methodologies to create data-driven innovation and discovery.

Tools And Techniques In Biotechnology:

1. PCR Chain Reaction:

Describe polymerase chain reaction (PCR), a technique for amplifying particular DNA sequences. Explain the PCR process, including the usage of thermostable DNA polymerases and the phases of denaturation, annealing, and extension. Emphasise the uses of PCR in gene cloning, forensics, diagnostics, and molecular biology research.

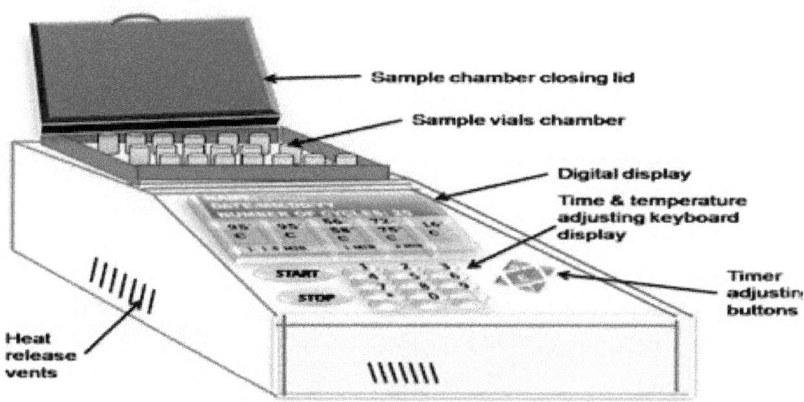

2. Recombinant DNA technology and gene cloning:

The process of isolating and reproducing particular DNA sequences in bacterial or yeast hosts is known as gene cloning. Talk about the steps involved in gene cloning, including DNA ligation, transformation, restriction enzyme digestion, and selection. Describe the uses of recombinant DNA technology in genetic engineering, protein synthesis, and gene expression.

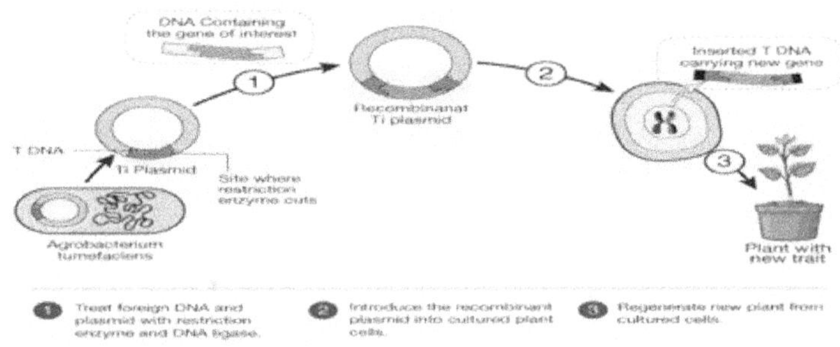

3. DNA Sequence

Describe DNA sequencing as the procedure used to ascertain the nucleotide base order within a DNA molecule. Explain the many techniques for sequencing DNA, such as third-generation sequencing technologies, next-generation sequencing (NGS), and Sanger sequencing. Talk about how DNA sequencing is used in genetic diagnoses, genome analysis, evolutionary biology, and personalised medicine.

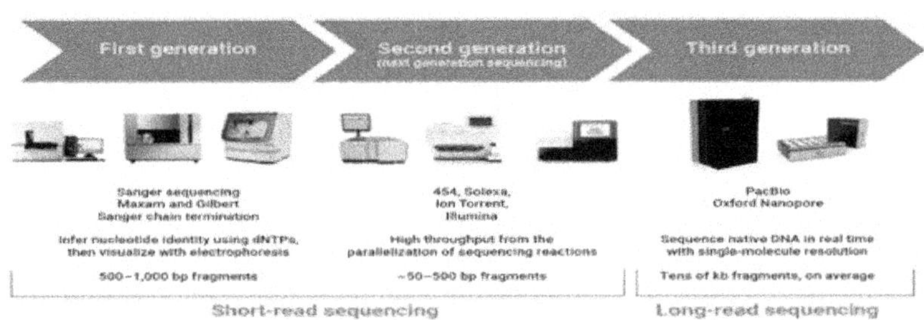

4. Methods of Gene Editing:

Describe gene editing as the exact alteration of the genome's DNA sequences. Talk about the fundamentals and uses of gene editing methods such zinc-finger nucleases, TALENs, and CRISPR-Cas9. Emphasise the potential applications of gene editing in basic science, agricultural biotechnology, and therapeutic interventions.

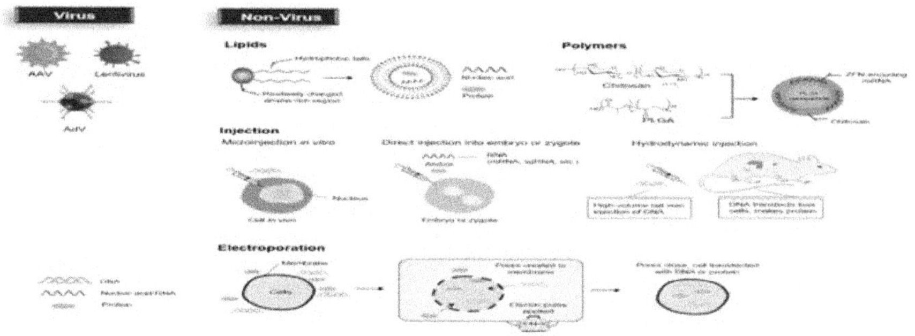

5.Protein Expression and Purification:

Generate recombinant proteins in host organisms like yeast, bacteria, or mammalian cells through the process of protein expression. Talk about the methods used to produce proteins, such as protein tagging, promoter regulation, and plasmid-based expression systems. Describe the uses of protein purification techniques like affinity, electrophoresis, and chromatography in structural biology and biopharmaceutical manufacturing.

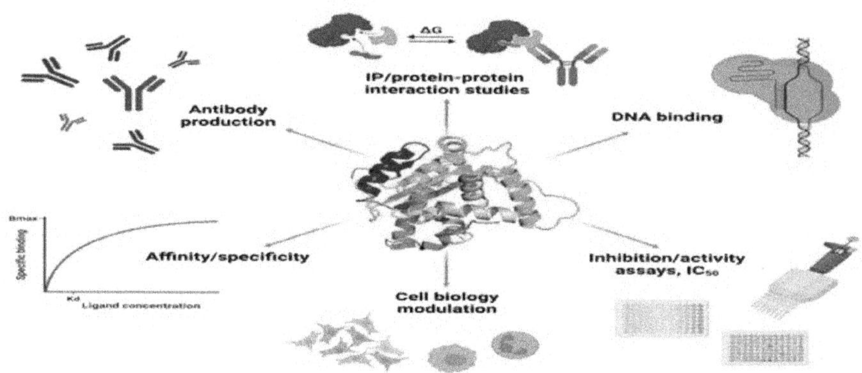

6. Cell Culture and Fermentation:

Cell culture is the regulated in vitro growth and maintenance of cells. Explain the methods and tools used in cell culture, such as incubators, culture media, cell lines, and bioreactors. Talk about the uses of fermentation and cell culture in the creation of biopharmaceuticals, the creation of vaccines, tissue engineering, and stem cell research.

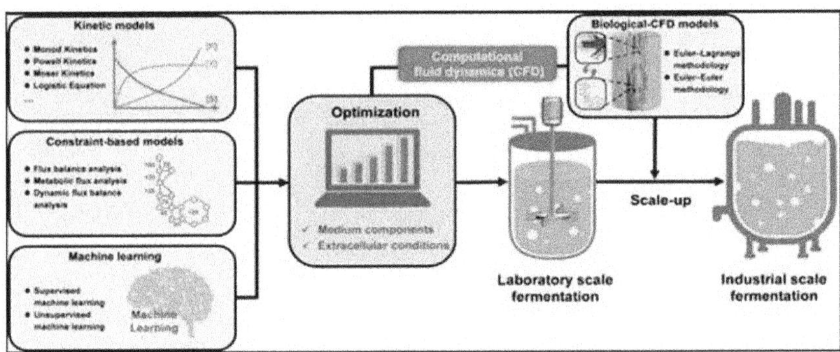

7. Tools and Databases for Bioinformatics:

Bioinformatics is the study of biological data analysis through the use of computational techniques. Talk about databases and bioinformatics tools for pathway analysis, genomic annotation, protein structure prediction, and sequence analysis. Emphasise how bioinformatics is used in drug development, personalised medicine, and genetic research. It can also be integrated with experimental procedures in systems biology approaches.

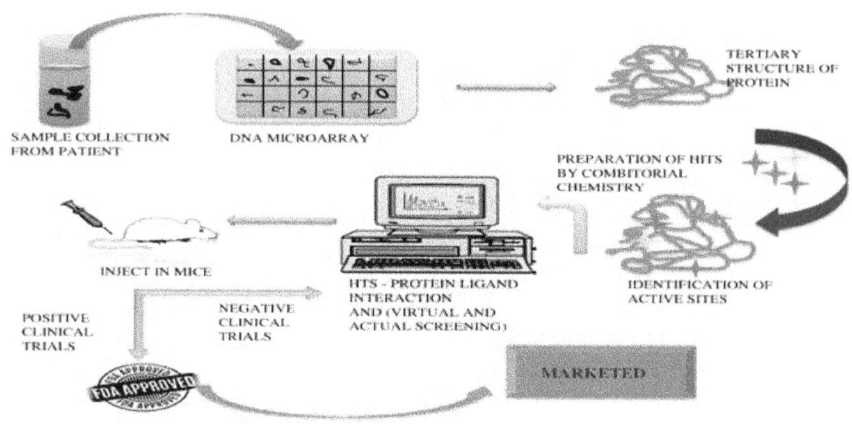

8. High-Throughput (HTS) Screening:

Describe HTS as a technique for quickly determining a certain biological activity of a huge number of chemicals or genetic variations. Explain the technology utilised in HTS, such as next-generation sequencing platforms, microarray-based assays, and automated liquid handling systems. Talk about the uses of HTS in systems biology, functional genomics, and drug discovery.

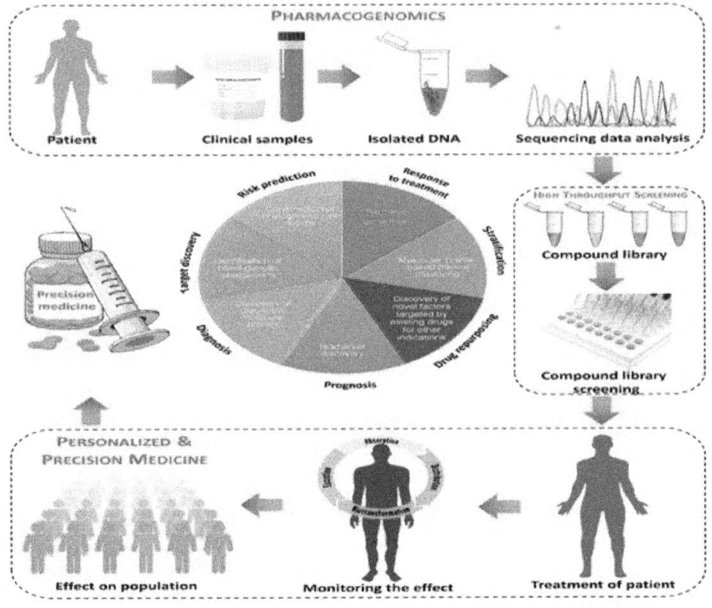

9. Flow Cytometry and Fluorescence Microscopy:

Introduce flow cytometry as a method for examining and classifying individual cells according to their physical and biological characteristics. This technique can also be used in conjunction with fluorescence microscopy. Explain how fluorescent labels are used in fluorescence microscopy to visualise biological structures and processes. Talk about the uses of fluorescence microscopy and flow cytometry in drug discovery, immunology, cell biology, and cancer research.

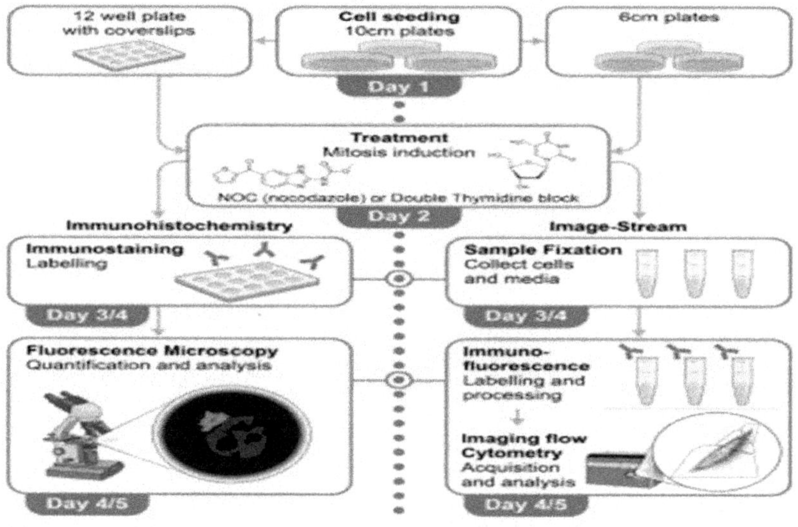

10. MS, or mass spectrometry:

Describe mass spectrometry as a method for using ionisation and fragmentation patterns to determine a molecule's mass and structure. Explain the various kinds of mass spectrometers, such as quadrupole, ion trap, and time-of-flight (TOF) devices. Talk about the use of mass spectrometry in structural biology, proteomics, metabolomics, and lipidomics, as well as how it may be combined with other omics technologies to provide thorough molecular analysis.

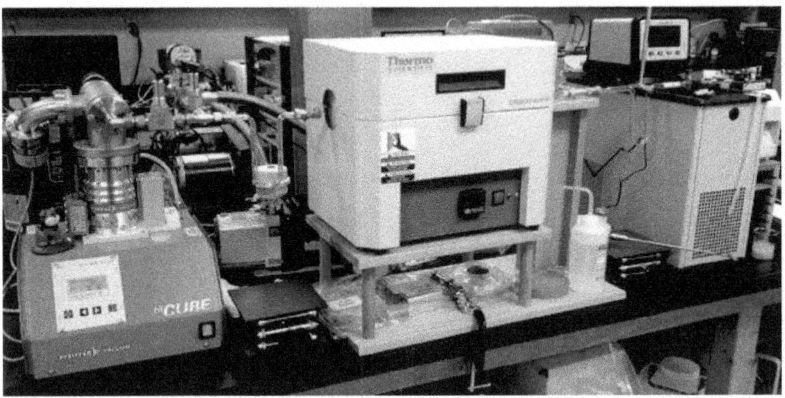

Ethical, Legal, and Social Implications:

- **Ethical Implications:**

1. Responsible Conduct of Research:
This section discusses the moral issues that accompany the ethical conduct of biotechnology research, such as accountability, transparency, and scientific integrity. In order to guarantee the validity and dependability of scientific findings, it is crucial to follow ethical norms and principles when designing experiments, gathering data, and reporting results.

2. Human subjects protection and informed consent:
Ethical issues with human subjects protection and informed consent in biotechnological research with human subjects. It is crucial to get research participants' voluntary, informed consent while also protecting their autonomy, privacy, and secrecy and reducing any risks or negative effects.

3. Animal Welfare and Research Ethics:
This section discusses the moral issues surrounding the use of animals in biotechnological research, such as humane treatment standards, animal welfare principles, and ethical guidelines for animal testing. Minimising animal suffering, providing suitable housing, care, and handling, and abiding by moral principles and laws controlling animal experimentation are all crucial.

- **Legal Implications:**
- **1. Regulatory Oversight And Compliance:**

The legal frameworks and rules that control the creation, research, and commercialization of biotechnology, particularly those pertaining to environmental protection, biosafety, and biosecurity. The significance of following legal and ethical guidelines, getting authorization, licences, and approvals, and complying with regulations when engaging in biotechnological operations.

2. Intellectual Property Rights:
This section discusses the legal aspects of biotechnology intellectual property rights, including patents, copyrights, and proprietary rights related to discoveries, inventions, and developments. Understanding and defending intellectual property is crucial, as is obtaining patents, licencing contracts, and commercialization plans in order to promote innovation and encourage funding for biotechnological research.

3. Data Protection And Privacy:
Legal considerations surrounding data protection, privacy, and confidentiality in biotechnological research, including regulations governing the collection, storage, and use of genomic data. Importance of safeguarding individuals' privacy rights, ensuring data security, and complying with data protection laws and regulations to protect sensitive information and maintain public trust.

- **Social Implications:**
- **1. Equitable Access And Social Justice:**

Addressing inequalities in healthcare access and research opportunities, as well as social issues pertaining to fair access to scientific knowledge, healthcare services, and biotechnological advancements. In order to guarantee that everyone in society may benefit from biotechnology, it is critical to advance social justice, inclusivity, and diversity in biotechnological research, outreach, and education.

2. **Public Engagement And Trust:**

Social aspects of biotechnological research and applications that relate to public engagement, communication, and trust-building, such as promoting open communication, mutual understanding, and transparency among scientists, decision-makers, and the general public. To increase public confidence in biotechnology and its effects on society, it is critical to involve stakeholders, respond to public concerns, and encourage informed decision-making.

3. Cultural And Ethical Principles:

Social factors that may affect attitudes, beliefs, and perceptions of biotechnology include ethical principles, cultural diversity, and societal standards. In order to ensure responsible and culturally sensitive practices, it is crucial that biotechnology research, development, and deployment recognise cultural distinctions, ethical principles, and community values.

Future Prospects:

1. Synthetic Biology And Genome Engineering:

By making it possible to create unique biological systems with specialised functions, advances in these fields are predicted to completely transform biotechnology. Biosensors, engineered gene circuits, and programmable genetic circuits are examples of synthetic biology techniques that show potential for use in the fields of environmental sustainability, energy, healthcare, and agriculture.

2. Gene Editing And CRISPR-Based Therapies:

CRISPR-based genome editing technologies, such CRISPR-Cas9, have the potential to revolutionise medicine by providing precise and focused treatments for infectious diseases, cancer, and hereditary illnesses. Improved delivery strategies, increased specificity, and broader uses in gene control, epigenome editing, and synthetic biology could be future advancements in CRISPR-based therapeutics.

3. Precision Agriculture And Personalised Medicine:

Biotechnology will advance personalised medicine, which uses patient data, biomarkers, and genetic information to customise treatments and interventions to each patient's particular needs. Similar to this, data-driven decision-making can be used to maximise crop yield, resource usage efficiency, and sustainability through precision agriculture technologies including genomic selection, precision breeding, and digital farming tools.

4. **Regenerative Medicine And Tissue Engineering:**

By utilising stem cells, biomaterials, and tissue engineering techniques to replace or repair damaged tissues and organs, these fields of study hold promise for meeting unmet medical needs. The creation of bioengineered organs, 3D bioprinting techniques, and customised tissue implants for transplantation and restorative treatments are possible future developments in regenerative medicine.

5. **Future Research Efforts In Microbiome:**

Science and microbial biotechnology will be fueled by the critical roles that the human microbiome and microbial communities play in health, disease, and environmental sustainability. Future uses could include microbial bioprocesses for the sustainable production of chemicals, minerals, and fuels as well as microbiome-based therapies, diagnostics, and interventions for a range of illnesses.

6. **Science of Data And Bioinformatics:**
Data science, bioinformatics, and computational biology methods to the analysis, interpretation, and modelling of complex biological data will play an increasingly important role in the future of biotechnology. Systems biology, drug development, and biomarker discovery will all benefit from researchers' ability to glean valuable insights from massive genomic, proteomic, and metabolomic datasets thanks to developments in machine learning, artificial intelligence, and big data analytics.

7. **Emerging Technologies And Convergence:**

The coming together of several fields, including as information technology, materials science, and nanotechnology, may influence the direction of biotechnology in the future by fostering the creation of new technologies and interdisciplinary approaches. Nanobiotechnology, quantum biology, and bio-inspired materials are examples of emerging technologies that have the potential to revolutionise biomedicine, nanomedicine, and sustainable manufacturing.

8. **Implications For Ethics, Law, And Society (ELSI):**
   Addressing the ethical, legal, and societal ramifications of concerns including genetic discrimination, data privacy, environmental damage, and fair access to biotechnological advancements will be crucial as biotechnology develops. Future initiatives will concentrate on creating legal guidelines, public participation plans, and ethical frameworks to guarantee the ethical and fair application of biotechnological developments for the good of society.

Conclusion:

1. Finally, the first chapter of a book on biotechnology acts as a starting point for readers to learn about this enormous and ever-expanding field by giving them background information, a sense of the past, and an outlook on the future. We have examined the many facets of biotechnology in this chapter, including its definition, application, underlying theories, methods, and ethical, legal, and societal ramifications.

2. Fundamentally, biotechnology is the use of biological concepts and methods to solve societal issues, boost food security, improve human health, and encourage environmental sustainability. The history of biotechnology has been characterised by historic discoveries, cutting-edge scientific advancements, and revolutionary applications in a wide range of fields, from prehistoric fermentation techniques to contemporary genome editing technologies

3. Biotechnology has the potential to completely transform industry, research, medicine, and agriculture in the years to come. Novel approaches like CRISPR-based gene editing, synthetic biology, personalised medicine, and regenerative medicines have the potential to solve urgent global concerns and open up new areas of research and development.

4. But these opportunities also bring with them social, legal, and ethical issues that need to be properly considered. The conscientious and just application of biotechnological innovations necessitates careful consideration, moral examination, and constructive discussion to guarantee that advantages are optimised, hazards are reduced, and the consequences are distributed fairly throughout the community.

5. Finally, the introduction chapter invites readers to investigate the science, technology, and sociological ramifications of this quickly developing discipline, setting the stage for an exciting voyage into the realm of biotechnology. We can leverage the power of biotechnology to address some of the most important issues confronting humanity and create a more sustainable and fair future for future generations by promoting curiosity, critical thinking, and interdisciplinary collaboration.

References

1. "Introduction to Biotechnology" by William J. Thieman and Michael A. Palladino - This textbook provides a comprehensive overview of the principles, applications, and ethical considerations of biotechnology, making it an excellent resource for introductory studies.

2. "Principles of Biotechnology" by Harisha Sridhar Shelat - This book covers the fundamentals of biotechnology, including molecular biology, genetic engineering, and bioprocessing, with a focus on practical applications and emerging trends.

3. "Biotechnology: An Introduction" by Susan R. Barnum - This introductory textbook offers a broad overview of biotechnology, including its historical development, scientific principles, and contemporary applications in medicine, agriculture, and industry.

4. "Biotechnology for Beginners" by Reinhard Renneberg, Arnold L. Demain, and Dieter Antranikian - This accessible introduction to biotechnology provides a comprehensive overview of key concepts, techniques, and applications, suitable for students and general readers.

5. "Introduction to Biotechnology" by Thierry G. M. J. van Kempen - This textbook covers the fundamentals of biotechnology, including molecular biology, genetic engineering, and bioprocess engineering, with an emphasis on real-world examples and case studies.

6. "Biotechnology: Science for the New Millennium" by Ellyn Daugherty - This introductory textbook explores the diverse applications of biotechnology in agriculture, healthcare, environmental science, and industry, highlighting the interdisciplinary nature of the field.

7. "Biotechnology: An Introduction" by Naveen Kumar Arora - This book provides a concise introduction to biotechnology, covering topics such as recombinant DNA technology, genomics, proteomics, and bioinformatics, with an emphasis on recent advances and future prospects.

8. "Introduction to Biotechnology" by M. K. Sateesh - This introductory textbook offers a comprehensive overview of biotechnology, including its historical background, scientific principles, and ethical considerations, making it suitable for students and educators alike.

9. "Biotechnology: An Illustrated Primer" by Rolf D. Schmid, Peter Döring, and Dietmar Schomburg - This illustrated guide provides an accessible introduction to biotechnology, covering topics such as genetic engineering, protein expression, and industrial bioprocesses, with informative graphics and illustrations.

10. "Biotechnology: Introduction and Perspectives" edited by Kirsi-Marja Oksman-Caldentey and Wolfgang H. Barz - This comprehensive textbook features contributions from leading experts in the field, covering a wide range of topics in biotechnology, from basic principles to advanced applications and societal implications.

CHAPTER TWO

UNLOCKING NATURE'S BLUEPRINT: THE POWER OF GENETIC ENGINEERING

Definition and Purpose:

Definition:

Genetic engineering is the intentional alteration of an organism's genetic makeup to produce particular characteristics or results.

Purpose:

- Promote Scientific Knowledge Through genetic engineering, scientists can investigate how genes work and how they relate to biological processes.
- Technological innovation: It provides a framework for creating novel instruments, methods, and technologies for a range of uses.
- Handle Societal Challenges: Genetic engineering holds promise for addressing a range of concerns, including those pertaining to environmental sustainability, food security, and health.
- Enhance Quality of Life: Genetic engineering helps to improve human well-being by creating lucrative biotechnological goods, increasing food yields, and creating therapies for genetic illnesses.

Historical Background:

1. **Progenitors:** The origins of genetic engineering can be found in traditional agricultural methods, such as the selective breeding of plants

and animals to improve desired characteristics. Nevertheless, these techniques did not directly manipulate genes; instead, they depended on natural variation.

2. **Discovery of DNA:** James Watson and Francis Crick's 1953 clarification of the DNA molecule's structure marked a turning point. The basis for comprehending the storage and transmission of genetic information was established by this revolutionary finding.

3. **Recombinant DNA Technology:** The advent of recombinant DNA technology in genetic engineering was a major turning point in the 1970s. Scientists like Paul Berg invented this technology, which made it possible for researchers to splice DNA from many sources together to create recombinant molecules with unique genetic combinations.

4. **First Recombinant DNA Experiment:** In 1972, Paul Berg conducted the first successful recombinant DNA experiment, demonstrating the transfer of genes between unrelated organisms. This achievement laid the groundwork for subsequent advancements in genetic engineering.

5. **Gene Cloning:** Throughout the 1970s and 1980s, researchers refined techniques for gene cloning, enabling the isolation, amplification, and manipulation of specific genes. This opened up new possibilities for studying gene function and producing valuable proteins through genetic engineering.

6. **Development of Transgenic Organisms:** In the 1980s, scientists achieved another breakthrough with the creation of transgenic organisms—organisms containing genes from other species. This technology paved the way for applications in agriculture, medicine, and biotechnology.

7. **Emergence of Gene Editing:** The advent of gene editing technologies, such as CRISPR-Cas9, has transformed the area of genetic engineering in recent decades. These instruments provide previously unheard-of control over gene expression and function by enabling precise, targeted alterations to DNA.

8. **Ongoing Developments:** Genome editing, synthetic biology, and gene therapy are just a few of the areas where genetic engineering is still advancing quickly. These advancements show promise in tackling urgent issues including food security, healthcare, and environmental sustainability.

Fundamental Principles:

1. DNA Structure: DNA, or deoxyribonucleic acid, is the molecule that contains the genetic instructions necessary for every known living thing's growth, development, and reproduction. Consisting of nucleotides with the bases adenine (A), thymine (T), cytosine (C), and guanine (G), it is wrapped into a double helix shape around two long strands.

2. Gene Expression: The act of using a gene's instructions to create functioning gene products, including proteins, is known as gene expression. It involves two primary stages: translation, in which ribosomes decode the messenger RNA (mRNA) to generate a specific protein, and transcription, in which a gene's DNA sequence is translated into an mRNA molecule.

3. Central Dogma of Molecular Biology: The movement of genetic information throughout a biological system is described by the basic dogma of molecular biology. It says that genetic information is translated (from DNA to RNA) and then transferred (by translation) from RNA to protein.

4. Genetic Modification: Introducing, removing, or changing particular DNA sequences can change an organism's genetic composition. Numerous methods, including gene editing (e.g., CRISPR-Cas9), gene insertion, deletion, and silence, can be used to accomplish this.

5. Recombinant DNA Technology: Through the manipulation of DNA molecules from various sources, new genetic combinations can be created. Restrictions enzymes are used to cut DNA at specified locations, splice DNA fragments together, and then insert the recombinant DNA into the host organism.

6. Gene Cloning: The act of creating several copies of a certain gene or DNA sequence is known as "gene cloning." The general procedure for this is to insert the desired DNA fragment into a vector (such a plasmid or viral genome), which acts as a carrier to deliver the DNA to host cells for replication.

7. Techniques for Modifying and Manipulating Genetic Material: Genetic engineering includes a variety of methods and instruments for modifying and manipulating genetic material. These include gel electrophoresis for separating DNA fragments, PCR (polymerase chain reaction) for amplifying DNA, and different gene editing technologies for precise genome modifications.

Techniques and Tools

1.Polymerase Chain Reaction (PCR): The method known as polymerase chain reaction, or PCR, is used to amplify particular DNA sequences. It uses a heat-stable DNA polymerase enzyme to cycle between primer annealing,

DNA denaturation, and DNA extension. In genetic engineering, PCR is frequently used for DNA cloning, sequencing, and analysis.

2. Restriction Enzymes:

Enzymes that recognise and cleave DNA at or near certain sequences are known as restriction enzymes, sometimes known as restriction endonucleases. They enable gene cloning, DNA modification, and recombinant DNA technologies by precisely cutting DNA at specific sites.

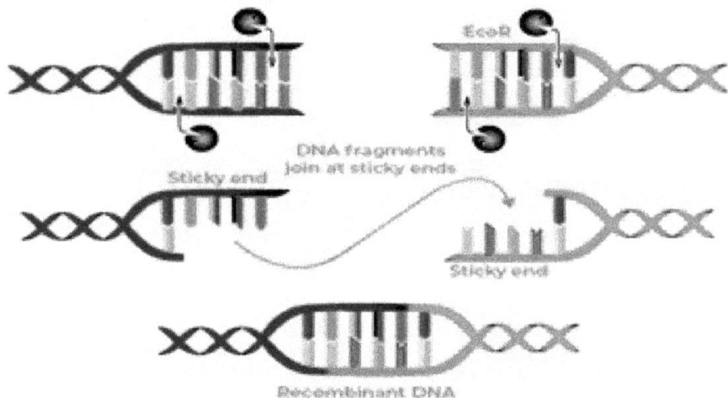

3. Cloning genes: Cloning genes entails inserting a targeted DNA fragment (the desired gene) into a vector, like the genome of a virus or plasmid. After being inserted into host cells, the recombinant DNA replicates alongside the host genome to produce multiple copies of the inserted gene.

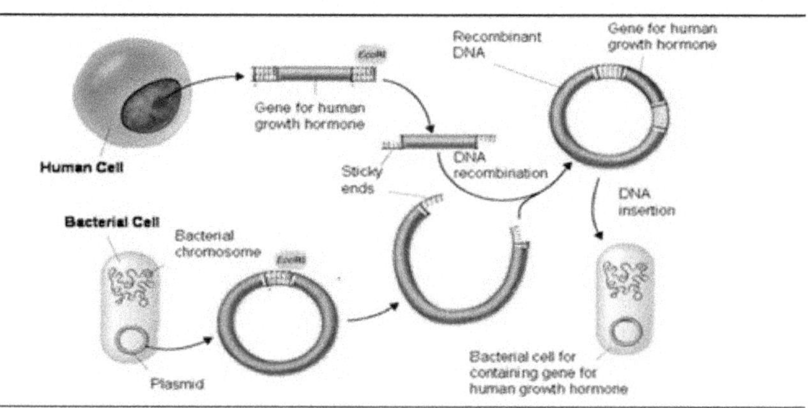

4. Gel electrophoresis:

It is a process that divides DNA fragments according to their charge and size. An electric field is used to force DNA molecules into wells of an agarose or polyacrylamide gel, where their size determines how quickly they migrate across the gel. Size estimate, fragment purification, and DNA analysis are all accomplished using gel electrophoresis.

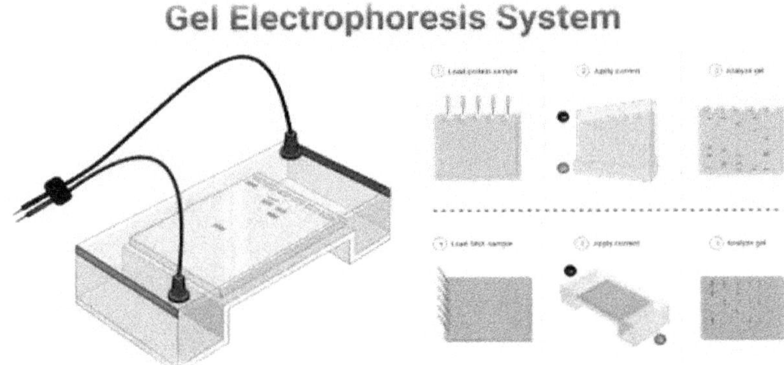

5. Gene editing technologies:

CRISPR-Cas9, TALENs, and zinc finger nucleases are a few examples of the technologies that allow for precise change of DNA sequences. With great efficiency and specificity, these instruments enable targeted genome editing, encompassing gene insertion, deletion, and alteration.

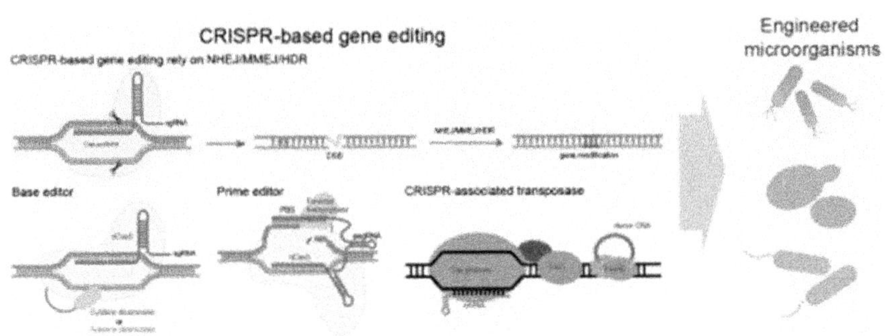

6. Reporter Assays:

Gene expression and regulation are studied using reporter assays. They entail the insertion of a reporter gene (such as GFP or luciferase) into animals or cells, which in response to the activity of regulatory elements or gene expression, produces a measurable output (such as fluorescence or luminescence).

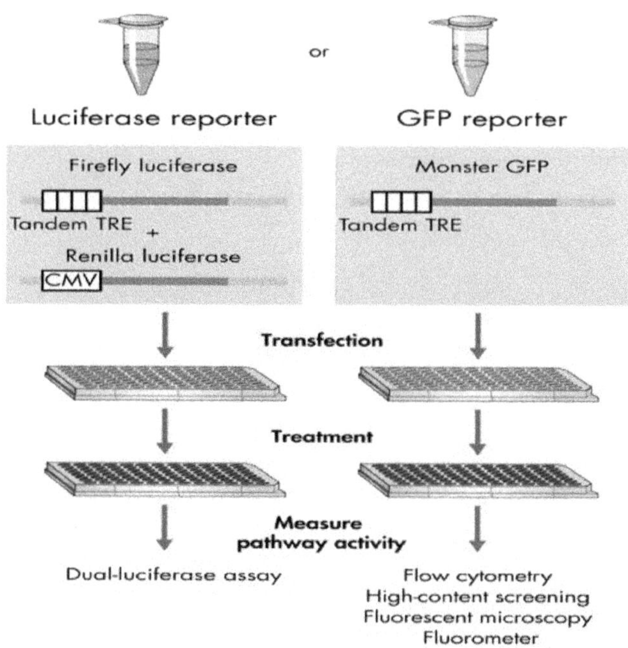

7. DNA Sequence:

The technique of ascertaining the exact nucleotide order within a DNA molecule is known as DNA sequencing. It makes it possible to identify genes, genetic variants, and mutations, as well as to clarify the genomic sequences of different organisms.

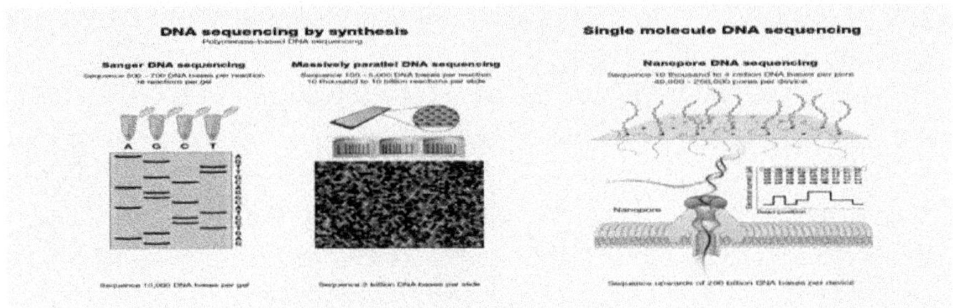

Applications

1. Medicine: Gene Therapy:

By inserting functioning genes into afflicted cells or tissues, genetic engineering is utilised to treat genetic illnesses.

Personalised medicine:

Based on a patient's genetic composition, medical interventions and treatments are customised using genetic information.

Drug Production:

Pharmaceutical medications, such as insulin and vaccinations, are produced by genetically modified organisms, such as yeast or bacteria.

2. Crops that have been genetically modified:

Herbicide resistance, pest resistance, and increased nutritional value are just a few of the desirable features that can be developed in crops by genetic engineering.

Crop Improvement:

In response to environmental problems, genetic modification techniques are used to increase crop yields, nutritional quality, and stress tolerance.

Enhancement of Livestock:

Through genetic engineering, desirable qualities in livestock can be bred, such as resistance to disease, faster development rates, and increased output of milk or meat.

3.Biotechnology:

Industrial Enzymes: Enzymes with specialised roles for industrial uses, like waste treatment, food processing, and biofuel production, are created by genetic engineering.

Bioremediation:

To help with environmental cleanup efforts, genetically modified microorganisms are used to break down pollutants and toxins in the environment.

Biopharmaceuticals:

Therapeutic proteins, antibodies, and vaccines for illness prevention and therapy are created by genetic engineering.

4. Research and Development:

Functional Genomics:

By using methods like gene deletion, knockdown, and overexpression, genetic engineering makes it possible to research the function and regulation of genes.

Model Organisms:

Human diseases, developmental processes, and biological systems are studied in genetically modified fruit flies and mice.

Synthetic Biology:

The discipline of synthetic biology is advanced via the use of genetic engineering in the design and construction of artificial biological systems with new functions and applications.

5. Environmental Conservation:

Biocontrol Agents:

To manage pests and diseases, biocontrol agents, such as genetically engineered bacteria or mosquitoes, are created using genetic engineering.

Conservation Genetics:

Genetic engineering methods are used to evaluate genetic variety, research and protect threatened species, and rebuild ecosystems.

Biotechnological Innovations

1. Industry Enzymes:

The manufacture of industrial enzymes, which are utilised in a variety of manufacturing processes, has been transformed via genetic engineering.

Enzymes that perform certain tasks, such lipases, amylases, proteases, and cellulases, are designed to improve stability, efficiency, and specificity.

These enzymes catalyse chemical reactions, break down complicated substrates, and increase product quality and yield in a variety of industries, including food and beverage, textiles, biofuels, pulp and paper, and detergents.

2. Biopharmaceuticals:

The development of medicinal proteins, antibodies, vaccines, and gene therapies is largely dependent on genetic engineering.

Utilising recombinant DNA technology, physiologically active proteins with therapeutic or diagnostic uses can be engineered into host cells, including bacteria, yeast, mammalian cells, and plants.

Biopharmaceuticals provide patients with targeted and individualised therapy choices for a wide range of ailments, including cancer, autoimmune disorders, infectious diseases, genetic disorders, and uncommon diseases.

3. Biofuels:

By maximising microbial or plant-based systems for biomass conversion and biofuel generation, genetic engineering helps to generate sustainable biofuels.

The effective conversion of renewable feedstocks, such as lignocellulosic biomass or algae biomass, into biofuels, such as ethanol, biodiesel, and biohydrogen, is achieved by engineering microorganisms, such as bacteria, yeast, and algae.

Improved metabolic pathways, resistance to inhibitors, and higher biomass output are examples of engineered features that boost the economic feasibility and efficiency of biofuel production processes, lowering reliance on fossil fuels and lessening environmental effects.

4. Bioremediation:

By using microorganisms to break down or detoxify pollutants and toxins, genetic engineering provides novel approaches to environmental cleanup.

Heavy metals, pesticides, industrial chemicals, petroleum hydrocarbons, and other environmental pollutants can all be broken down and detoxified by engineered bacteria, fungus, or plants.

Through the restoration of ecosystems, preservation of public health, and mitigation of environmental pollution and degradation, bioremediation technologies clean up contaminated soil, water, and air.

5. Biological Manufacturing:

By employing renewable biological resources, genetic engineering makes it possible to create biological manufacturing platforms that produce materials, chemicals, and consumer goods.

In order to biosynthesize important substances, such as bio-based polymers, specialised chemicals, flavours, perfumes, and cosmetics, microorganisms like yeast or bacteria are modified.

As an eco-friendly and sustainable substitute for conventional chemical synthesis techniques, biological manufacturing technologies minimise waste production, cut carbon emissions, and lessen dependency on fossil fuels.

Future Directions

1. Synthetic Biology:

To create and build unique biological systems with specialised purposes, synthetic biology is an interdisciplinary method that incorporates concepts from computer science, molecular biology, genetic engineering, and engineering. Future developments in synthetic biology could result in the creation of biological circuits, programmable cells, and synthetic organisms with uses in biotechnology, medicine, and other fields.

2. Advanced Genome Editing Technologies:

Advances in accuracy, effectiveness, and adaptability have led to the continued evolution of genome editing techniques, including CRISPR-Cas9. In order to precisely manipulate genetic material, future directions include developing next-generation genome editing techniques with improved specificity, multiplexing capabilities, and less off-target effects.

3. Gene drives:

Within populations, certain genetic features can spread quickly due to the biassing of one's own inheritance via gene drives. Gene drives may be used in the future for disease eradication, pest control, and conservation initiatives, but ethical and ecological issues need to be carefully considered.

4. Precision Medicine:

Precision medicine aims to tailor medical treatments and interventions to individual patients based on their genetic makeup, lifestyle factors, and environmental exposures. Future directions include the integration of genomic data, biomarkers, and advanced diagnostics to optimize treatment strategies, improve patient outcomes, and prevent disease.

5. Gene therapy:

By repairing or replacing damaged genes, gene therapy shows promise in the treatment of cancer, acquired diseases, and hereditary disorders.

The creation of safer and more effective delivery methods, enhanced gene editing methods, and customised gene therapy strategies are some of the future directions.

6. Biological Engineering:

The field of biological engineering is concerned with the development of biological systems for real-world uses. The creation of bio-based materials, bioinspired technologies, and biohybrid devices with uses in materials science, energy, environmental remediation, and medicine are some of the future directions in this field.

7. Ethical and Social Implications:

It's critical to address ethical, social, and regulatory issues as genetic engineering technologies develop.

In order to guarantee responsible innovation, egalitarian access to genetic technology, and transparent governance, future directions include continuing discourse, public participation, and interdisciplinary collaboration.

References

1. Watson, J.D., Baker, T.A., Bell, S.P., Gann, A., Levine, M., & Losick, R. (2013). Molecular Biology of the Gene (7th ed.). Cold Spring Harbor Laboratory Press.

1. Setlow, J.K. (Ed.). (2011). Genetic Engineering: Principles and Methods (Volume 33). Springer.

3. Setlow, J.K. (2015). Genetic Engineering: Principles, Procedures, and Consequences (4th ed.). Springer.

4. Doudna, J.A., & Charpentier, E. (2014). The new frontier of genome engineering with CRISPR-Cas9. Science, 346(6213), 1258096. https://doi.org/10.1126/science.1258096

5. Jinek, M., Chylinski, K., Fonfara, I., Hauer, M., Doudna, J.A., & Charpentier, E. (2012). A programmable dual-RNA-guided DNA endonuclease in adaptive bacterial immunity. Science, 337(6096), 816-821. https://doi.org/10.1126/science.1225829

6. Gaj, T., Gersbach, C.A., & Barbas III, C.F. (2013). ZFN, TALEN, and CRISPR/Cas-based methods for genome engineering. Trends in Biotechnology, 31(7), 397-405. https://doi.org/10.1016/j.tibtech.2013.04.004

7. Cong, L., Ran, F.A., Cox, D., Lin, S., Barretto, R., Habib, N., ... & Zhang, F. (2013). Multiplex genome engineering using CRISPR/Cas systems. Science, 339(6121), 819-823. https://doi.org/10.1126/science.1231143

8. Hsu, P.D., Lander, E.S., & Zhang, F. (2014). Development and applications of CRISPR-Cas9 for genome engineering. Cell, 157(6), 1262-1278. https://doi.org/10.1016/j.cell.2014.05.010

9. Jinek, M., East, A., Cheng, A., Lin, S., Ma, E., & Doudna, J. (2013). RNA-programmed genome editing in human cells. eLife, 2, e00471. https://doi.org/10.7554/eLife.00471

10. National Human Genome Research Institute (NHGRI). (n.d.). Retrieved from https://www.genome.gov/

11. European Molecular Biology Organization (EMBO). (n.d.). Retrieved from https://www.embo.org/

12. CRISPR-Associated (Cas) Gene Databases. (n.d.). Retrieved from https://www.addgene.org/crispr/cas9/

CHAPTER THREE

REVOLUTIONIZING MEDICINE: THE RISE OF BIOPHARMACEUTICALS

Introduction To Biopharmaceuticals

Pharmaceuticals made from biological sources, such as live things or their constituent parts like proteins, nucleic acids, or cells, are known as biopharmaceuticals. They represent a broad spectrum of therapeutic modalities, including gene therapies, cell-based treatments, monoclonal antibodies, and vaccinations, and they differ from conventional small molecule medications.

Biopharmaceuticals cover a wide range of diseases and provide creative answers to difficult medical problems. They offer chances for highly individualised and focused therapy, which may enhance patient results and quality of life. Furthermore, biopharmaceuticals support improvements in illness management, preventative medicine, and the creation of cutting-edge therapeutic approaches.

The development of biopharmaceuticals can be attributed to significant findings made in the middle of the 20th century, when basic studies in genetics and molecular biology prepared the way for their later creation. These early discoveries paved the way for later discoveries by providing the framework for comprehending the basic mechanics behind biological activity.

The development of recombinant DNA technology in the 1970s marked a major advancement. Through the use of this revolutionary method, scientists were able to modify genetic material and introduce genes from one organism into the DNA of another. This breakthrough opened the door to an unparalleled level of therapeutic protein manufacturing, ushering in a new era in medical history.

A significant turning point in the biopharmaceutical industry's history occurred in 1982 when the FDA approved recombinant human insulin. This was the first time recombinant DNA technology was successfully used for commercial purposes in the medical field. Insulin was previously obtained from animal pancreases, but recombinant technology provided a more dependable and safe substitute, completely changing the way diabetes is treated around the globe.

The biotechnology industry grew at an exponential rate throughout the 1980s and 1990s. Encouraged by developments in molecular biology and genetic engineering, businesses started making significant investments in biopharmaceutical R&D. During this time, a large number of biotech companies were founded with the goal of using biopharmaceuticals to solve unmet medical needs.

Revolutionizing Medicine: The Rise of Biopharmaceuticals" introduces the transformative impact of biopharmaceuticals on modern healthcare. This concept embodies a paradigm shift in therapeutic approaches, where medicinal products derived from biological sources—ranging from proteins and nucleic acids to living cells—have revolutionized the treatment landscape. This introduction explores the historical context, technological innovations, therapeutic applications, and future prospects of biopharmaceuticals, highlighting their pivotal role in addressing unmet medical needs, driving precision medicine, and reshaping the pharmaceutical industry. Through a comprehensive exploration of the rise of biopharmaceuticals, this narrative underscores their profound influence on advancing patient care, shaping healthcare delivery, and charting the course for a new era of medical innovation.

Biotechnological Innovations

1. Recombinant DNA Technology:

Examine the advancements made in recombinant DNA technology, which enable researchers to splice DNA from one organism into another. Emphasise how important it is for biopharmaceuticals, as it makes it possible for host organisms like yeast or bacteria to produce therapeutic proteins.

2. Monoclonal Antibody Technology:

Talk about the development of monoclonal antibody technology, which makes it possible to produce extremely specific antibodies that are directed against certain antigens. Give examples of its uses in biopharmaceuticals, such as the creation of cancer, autoimmune, and infectious disease-specific monoclonal antibody medications.

3. Protein Engineering:

Describe the basic ideas behind protein engineering, which is creating and altering proteins to have certain purposes or characteristics. Examine how the creation of innovative biopharmaceuticals with enhanced efficacy, stability, and safety characteristics has been made possible via protein engineering.

4. Technologies for Gene Editing:

Describe the most recent developments in gene editing tools, including zinc-finger nucleases, TALENs, and CRISPR-Cas9. Talk about their possible uses in the study of genetic disorders, genome editing for medicinal purposes, and gene therapy in biopharmaceutical research.

5. Bioprocessing Techniques:

Talk about the fermentation, cell culture, and downstream purification processes that are employed in the manufacturing of biopharmaceuticals. Emphasise bioprocessing technological advancements that aim to lower production costs, improve product quality, and increase yield.

6. Omics Technologies:

Investigate the application of omics technologies (genomics, transcriptomics, proteomics, and metabolomics) in the study and creation of biopharmaceuticals. Talk about the applications of omics data in defining pharmacological targets, comprehending disease mechanisms, and tailoring therapeutic strategies.

Therapeutic Applications

1. Monoclonal Antibody Therapies:

The use of monoclonal antibodies for targeted therapy in situations including cancer, autoimmune diseases, and infectious diseases should be discussed. Emphasise particular monoclonal antibody medications and their modes of action, such as infliximab for rheumatoid arthritis and rituximab for lymphoma.

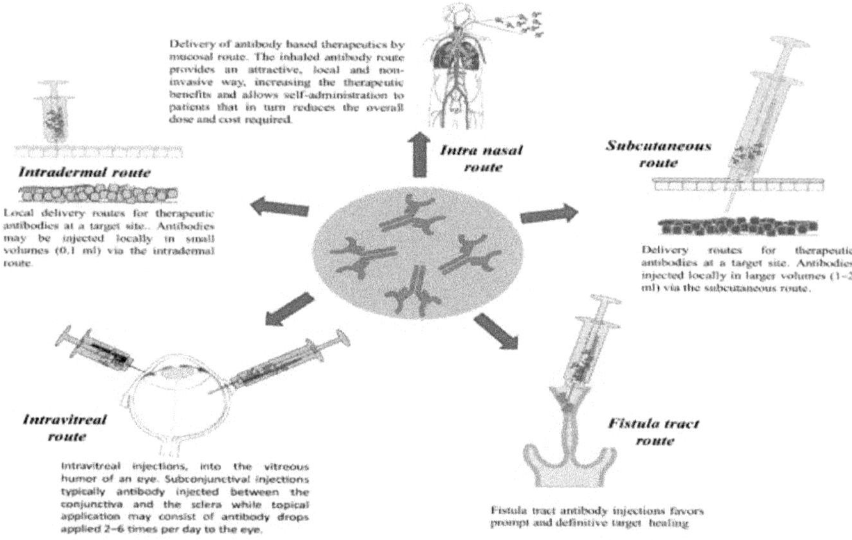

2. Gene Therapies:

Investigate the use of gene therapy in the treatment of cancer, genetic abnormalities, and other illnesses.

Give instances of effective gene therapy treatments, such as CAR-T cell therapy for specific forms of leukaemia and lymphoma and Luxturna for hereditary retinal degeneration.

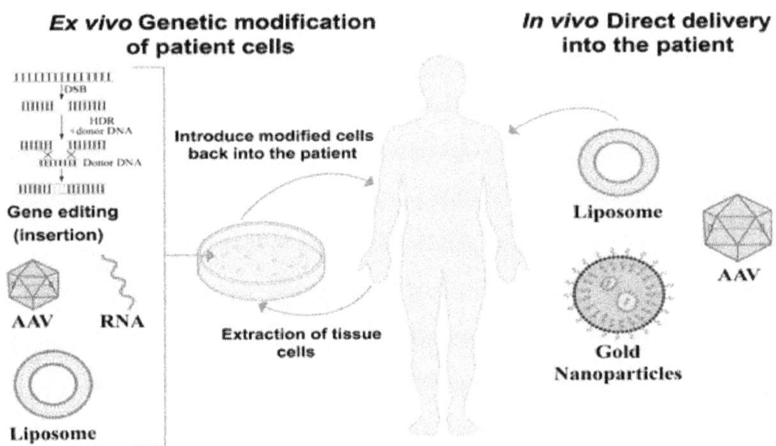

3. Vaccines:

The use of monoclonal antibodies for targeted therapy in situations including cancer, autoimmune diseases, and infectious diseases should be discussed. Emphasise particular monoclonal antibody medications and their modes of action, such as infliximab for rheumatoid arthritis and rituximab for lymphoma.

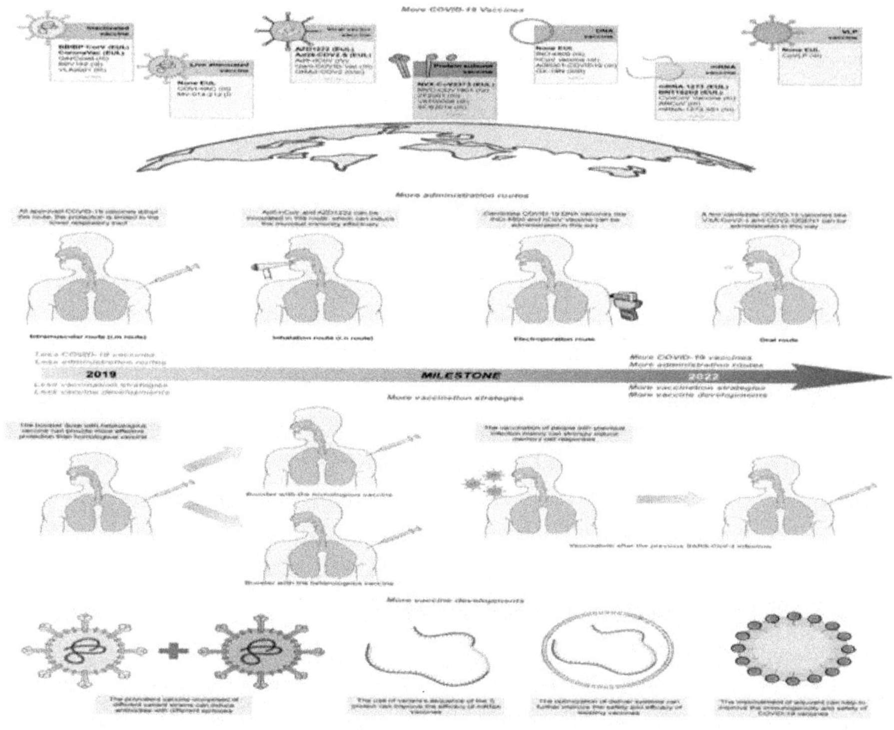

4. Cell-Based Therapies:

Investigate the use of gene therapy in the treatment of cancer, genetic abnormalities, and other illnesses. Give instances of effective gene therapy treatments, such as CAR-T cell therapy for specific forms of leukaemia and lymphoma and Luxturna for hereditary retinal degeneration.

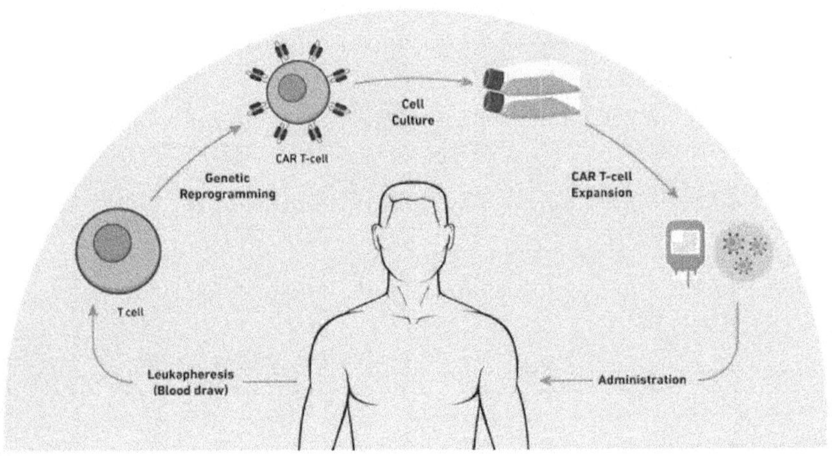

5. Nucleic Acid-Based Therapeutics:

Investigate the application of nucleic acid-based therapies, such as RNA interference (RNAi) and antisense oligonucleotides, in the treatment of genetic disorders and regulation of gene expression. Describe certain nucleic acid-based medications and their uses, such as patisiran for hereditary transthyretin amyloidosis and nusinersen for spinal muscular atrophy.

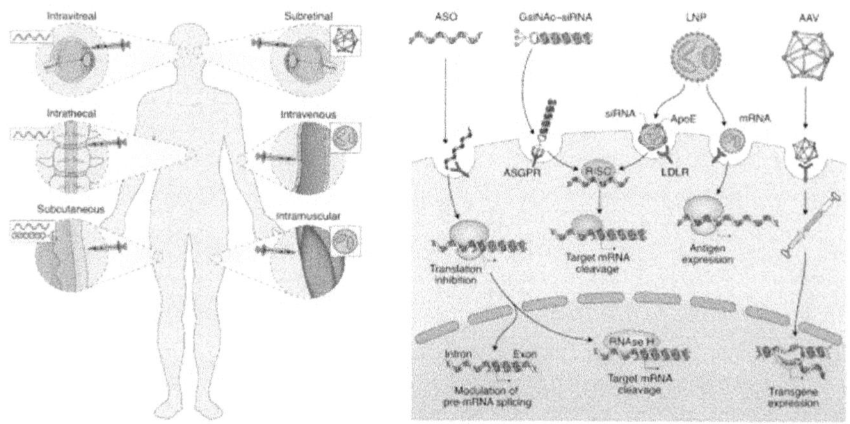

Advantages of Biopharmaceuticals

1. Tailored Therapies:

By precisely interacting with particular molecules or cell types implicated in disease processes, biopharmaceuticals provide highly tailored therapeutic methods. By minimising off-target effects and lowering the chance of adverse events, this tailored approach enhances patient safety and tolerability.

2. Decreased Side Effects:

Compared to conventional small molecule medications, biopharmaceuticals usually have fewer side effects because of their exact targeting and selective binding processes. Patient compliance and quality of life are improved by this decreased incidence of adverse effects, especially in chronic or long-term treatment regimens.

3. Personalised Medicine:

Treatments can be customised for each patient according to their genetic composition, the features of their illness, and other variables. Biopharmaceuticals show promise in this regard. By using a personalised approach, the chances of treatment resistance or non-response are reduced and treatment efficacy is maximised.

4. Complex Therapeutic Targets:

Biopharmaceuticals are an excellent choice for addressing therapeutic targets and intricate disease processes that are challenging to treat with traditional medications. They can interact with specific cell surface receptors, complex molecular pathways, and protein-protein interactions to enable new approaches to treating a variety of disorders.

5. Longer Half-Life and Duration of activity:

When compared to small molecule medications, many biopharmaceuticals have longer half-lives and longer durations of activity. This longer pharmacokinetic profile frequently makes it possible to schedule doses less frequently, which eases the burden of treatment and enhances patient convenience and adherence.

6. Possibility for Combination Therapies:

Synergistic therapy regimens can be created by combining biopharmaceuticals with other biologics or conventional medications. Because of its adaptability, combination medicines that target several disease pathways at once can be developed, improving therapeutic outcomes.

Challenges And Opportunities

1. Difficult Manufacturing Procedures:

Difficulties:

Biotechnological procedures, including cell culture, fermentation, and purification, are involved in the highly regulated, complex manufacturing processes of biopharmaceuticals.

Prospects:

Advances in manufacturing technologies, such continuous processing and single-use systems, present chances to boost productivity, cut expenses, and improve efficiency.

2. Regulatory Obstacles:

Difficulties:

In order to receive regulatory approval, biopharmaceuticals must meet strict standards for safety, efficacy, and quality.

Possibilities:

Industry players and regulatory bodies working together can promote the creation of simplified regulatory processes and hasten the approval of new biopharmaceutical products.

3. High Development Costs:

Difficulties:

The intricacy of research and development, along with the expenses related to manufacturing and clinical testing, make the development of biopharmaceuticals a financially demanding endeavour.

Opportunities:

To reduce financial barriers and encourage investment in biopharmaceutical innovation, strategic alliances, public-private partnerships, and creative funding models (such as venture capital and crowdsourcing) can be used.

4. Safety and Immunogenicity Concerns:

Difficulties:

Patients' immune systems may respond to biopharmaceuticals, which could result in negative side effects such hypersensitivity reactions or reduced medication efficacy.

Opportunities:

To reduce immunogenicity and improve the safety profile of biopharmaceuticals, developments in protein engineering, formulation optimisation, and immunomodulatory techniques are available.

5. Market Reimbursement and Access:

Difficulties:

Biopharmaceuticals may find it difficult to enter markets and get paid because of restrictions on market access, reimbursement guidelines, and pricing pressures.

Opportunities:

To ensure that biopharmaceutical medicines are affordable and accessible for patients, value-based pricing models, health technology assessments, and patient access programmes can help

optimise market access and reimbursement methods.

6. New Technologies and Treatment Approaches:

Obstacles:

The biopharmaceutical business has a range of opportunities and problems due to the rapid breakthroughs in biotechnology and the advent of novel therapeutic modalities. These issues include the need to adapt to new technologies and navigate regulatory considerations.

Opportunities:

Businesses can position themselves to take advantage of emerging markets and unmet medical needs by investing in the research and development of next-generation biopharmaceuticals, such as gene therapies, cell-based therapies, and RNA-based therapeutics.

Future Aspects

1. Biopharmaceutical Innovation:

New biopharmaceuticals with improved safety profiles, increased efficacy, and novel modes of action are anticipated to be developed as a result of ongoing biotechnology innovation. Developments in fields like gene editing, protein engineering, and omics technologies will make it possible to develop next-generation treatments that will address a variety of illnesses.

2. Personalised Medicine:

It is anticipated that developments in genomes, biomarker identification, and precision diagnostics will hasten the transition to personalised medicine. This paradigm shift will be largely facilitated by biopharmaceuticals, which will enable the development of customised treatments that are exactly matched to individual patients based on their genetic composition, disease features, and other variables.

3. Advanced Therapeutic Modalities:

New approaches to treating diseases, such as gene therapies, cell-based treatments, and RNA-based therapeutics, have the potential to completely change how people are treated for a wide range of illnesses, including cancer, uncommon diseases, and genetic disorders. These cutting-edge methods present the possibility of curative care and long-term advantages for patients.

4. Digital Health Integration:

More individualised and data-driven methods to drug development, clinical trials, and patient care will be made possible by the integration of digital health technologies, such as wearables, artificial intelligence, and big data analytics. These technologies will be used by biopharmaceutical businesses more frequently to streamline drug development procedures, find novel therapeutic targets, and track treatment results in real time.

5. Global Health Challenges:

Emerging pandemics, antibiotic resistance, and infectious illnesses are just a few of the issues that biopharmaceuticals will continue to be crucial in tackling. Global public health will be protected by the creation of vaccinations, antiviral medications, and biologics that target infectious agents in order to stop and manage future outbreaks.

6. Regulatory And Market Dynamic Landscape:

Biopharmaceutical innovation will need regulatory bodies and healthcare systems to adjust, striking a balance between the necessity of strict control and the pressing need to expedite access to life-saving medications. Future biopharmaceutical product commercialization and uptake will also be influenced by market factors, such as pricing pressures, reimbursement schemes, and market access issues.

References

1. Walsh, G. (2018). Biopharmaceuticals: Biochemistry and Biotechnology (3rd ed.). John Wiley & Sons.
2. This comprehensive textbook provides an in-depth overview of the biochemistry, biotechnology, and therapeutic applications of biopharmaceuticals.
3. Roberts, M. J., & Bentley, M. D. (2013). Biopharmaceuticals: Biochemistry and Biotechnology. John Wiley & Sons.
4. Another authoritative textbook covering the fundamental principles and cutting-edge developments in biopharmaceutical research and development.
5. Grabowski, H. G., & DiMasi, J. A. (2018). The economics of the biopharmaceutical industry. Journal of Economic Perspectives, 32(2), 139-160.
6. This article offers insights into the economic factors driving the growth of the biopharmaceutical industry and its impact on healthcare markets.
7. Aggarwal, S. R., & Whatcott, C. J. (2020). The Rise of Biopharmaceuticals: New Therapies, Increased Market Competition, and Changing Business Models. The Oncologist, 25(3), e555-e560.
8. This review article discusses the emergence of biopharmaceuticals as a major force in the pharmaceutical industry, focusing on new therapies, market dynamics, and business strategies.
9. Alliance for Regenerative Medicine. (2021). Regenerative Medicine and Advanced Therapies: The Year in Review. Retrieved from https://alliancerm.org/sector-report/alliance-2021-year-in-review/
10. This report provides an overview of the latest developments and trends in regenerative medicine and advanced therapies, including cell and gene therapies, which are reshaping the biopharmaceutical landscape.
11. European Medicines Agency. (2020). Biotechnology Medicines. Retrieved from https://www.ema.europa.eu/en/human-regulatory/overview/biotechnology-medicines-overview
12. The European Medicines Agency provides regulatory guidance and information on biotechnology medicines, offering insights into the

regulatory framework governing the development and approval of biopharmaceuticals in Europe.

CHAPTER FOUR

INDUSTRIAL BIOTECHNOLOGY: TRANSFORMING PROCESSES, PRODUCTS, AND PERSPECTIVES

INTRODUCTION

A silent revolution is happening in the world of modern industry, one that is being propelled by the complex dance of living things rather than the clang of machinery. The area of industrial biotechnology serves as an embodiment of this transition, which signifies a basic change in the way we conceptualise, create, and responsibly use the outcomes of human effort. Industrial biotechnology uses biology to transform processes, goods, and viewpoints in a variety of industries, including energy, environmental remediation, healthcare, and agriculture. Fundamental to it is the combination of engineering and biological sciences, which allows for the development of creative solutions that are both commercially and environmentally sustainable. This chapter takes us on a tour of the exciting field of industrial biotechnology, examining its foundational ideas, wide range of applications, recent technological developments, and future prospects and problems. We reveal the revolutionary potential of industrial biotechnology to design a future that is more robust, efficient, and equitable—from the fermentation vats of biorefineries to the synthetic biology labs. Come explore the complex web of industrial biotechnology with us. It is a web woven with the strands of creativity, teamwork, and the limitless potential of life to advance humankind into a better future. At the nexus of biology and industry, industrial biotechnology presents a novel approach to sustainable development and resource management. This subject, which has its roots in antiquated methods like brewing and fermentation, has developed into a vibrant one with the potential to transform conventional industrial processes and promote a bio-based economy.

Industrial biotechnology is changing our understanding of production, consumption, and waste management through the development of biofuels that lessen our need on fossil fuels and the fabrication of bio-based materials that have a minimal environmental impact. Its uses are extensive, affecting almost every facet of human endeavour and providing creative answers to some of our most urgent problems. Industrial biotechnology, which uses the amazing powers of microbes, enzymes, and biological systems to advance industrial processes, is fundamentally the fusion of human creativity with the inventiveness of nature. Industrial biotechnology has numerous and significant uses, ranging from the creation of biodegradable polymers to the creation of innovative medications. These applications offer environmentally friendly substitutes for traditional methods while also lessening our impact on the environment. However, the history of industrial biotechnology also tells a tale of cooperation and multidisciplinary synergy in addition to scientific discovery and technological success. To realise the full promise of biotechnology and push the envelope towards a more sustainable and just future, scientists, engineers, policymakers, and business titans collaborate across disciplinary barriers.

Few endeavours in human history have as much potential to shape our future as industrial biotechnology. This emerging discipline is a union of scientific excellence and industrial pragmatism, using the microscopic components of life to pave the way for a more wealthy, efficient, and sustainable society. Industrial biotechnology is a force for change that is transforming our knowledge of manufacturing, agriculture, healthcare, and environmental stewardship. It is more than just a scientific field. Its core is a deep respect for the complex machinery of life, as scientists and engineers collaborate with the natural world to discover its mysteries and realise its promise. Industrial biotechnology is a story of invention, cooperation, and limitless potential, from the busy fermenters of biorefineries to the clean labs of genetic engineers. It's a tale that cuts over boundaries and academic specialties, uniting bright people from all walks of life to work towards the same objective: using biology to solve some of the most important problems facing humanity.

FUNDAMENTALS OF INDUSTRIAL BIOTECHNOLOGY

Industrial biotechnology uses living things—plants, bacteria, and enzymes—to carry out particular tasks and generate useful goods. Fundamentally, industrial biotechnology maximises biological systems for use in industry by fusing ideas from engineering, chemistry, and biology.

Important Components of Industrial Biotechnology Consist of:

1. Biological Agents:

Because microorganisms can effectively transform raw materials into desirable products, such as bacteria, yeast, and fungi, they are frequently employed in industrial biotechnology. Biological catalysts like enzymes are essential for quickening metabolic reactions and are frequently used in industrial operations.

2. Bioprocess Engineering:

It is the design and optimisation of bioprocesses to produce desired molecules. This involves building fermentation or bioreactor systems for large-scale production, choosing appropriate microbial strains, and optimising growth parameters (such as temperature, pH, and nutrient availability).

3. Genetic Engineering:

Microbial strains can be modified by genetic engineering techniques to increase their productivity, increase their resistance to environmental stresses, or synthesise new chemicals. This could entail changing preexisting genes, adding genes from different organisms, or adjusting regulatory circuits.

4. Fermentation:

A key step in industrial biotechnology, fermentation is the controlled process by which microbes turn substrates—raw materials—into desirable products. Depending on the metabolic needs of the microbe and the intended result, fermentation can be either aerobic (requiring oxygen) or anaerobic (without oxygen).

5. Post-fermentation:

The target product is separated and purified from the fermentation broth using steps in the downstream processing sequence. To isolate the product from biomass and other contaminants, this may entail the use of filtration, centrifugation, chromatography, and precipitation tools.

6. Product diversification:

The manufacturing of a large range of goods, such as food additives, enzymes, biofuels, bioplastics, medicines, and specialised chemicals, is made possible by industrial biotechnology. Complex compounds with high specificity and efficiency can be synthesised thanks to the adaptability of biological systems.

7.Sustainability:

Using renewable resources, cutting down on waste production, and lowering dependency on fossil fuels are just a few of the ways that industrial biotechnology can help promote sustainability. Industrial biotechnology provides more environmentally friendly production alternatives to conventional techniques by utilising biological processes.

APPLICATIONS ACROSS INDUSTRIES

1. Agriculture:

Creation of genetically engineered crops that are more resilient to illnesses, pests, and environmental stressors.Production of insecticides, fertilisers, and biostimulants derived from plants in order to increase crop output and sustainability.

Application of microbial inoculants to promote nutrient cycling and soil health.

2. Health Care:

Manufacturing of biopharmaceuticals for the treatment of different illnesses, including as recombinant proteins, vaccines, and monoclonal antibodies. Creation of cell-based and gene therapies to treat hereditary illnesses and advance regenerative medicine. Use of bioprocessing methods to produce antibiotics, diagnostic reagents, and therapeutic enzymes.

3. Food and Drink:

bread, cheese, yoghurt, wine, beer, and other food and beverage goods produced through fermentation.

The use of enzymes in food processing can enhance its texture, flavour, and nutritional content.

food preservation, flavour enhancement, and probiotic supplementation using microbial cultures.

4. Energy:

Production of biofuels from renewable biomass feedstocks, such as bioethanol, biodiesel, and biogas.

using biorefinery techniques to transform lignocellulosic biomass into bio-based products, chemicals, and energy sources. Creation of microbial fuel cells to produce power from organic waste sources.

5. Environmental Remediation:

Bioremediation of contaminated soil and water environments using microbial consortia capable of degrading pollutants. Phytoextraction and phytoremediation techniques employing plants and microorganisms to remove heavy metals and organic contaminants. Wastewater treatment using biological processes, such as activated sludge treatment, anaerobic digestion, and constructed wetlands.

6. Textiles and Materials:

Production of bio-based polymers, such as polylactic acid (PLA) and polyhydroxyalkanoates (PHAs), for use in textiles, packaging, and biodegradable plastics. Enzymatic processes for textile processing, including desizing, scouring, bleaching, and dyeing, with reduced environmental impact.Utilization of bio-based fibers, such as bamboo, hemp, and lyocell, as sustainable alternatives to conventional textiles.

TECHNOLOGICAL ADVANCEMENTS

1. Synthetic Biology:

New biological systems with customised functionalities can be designed and built thanks to advances in synthetic biology. This covers the production of complex compounds and the engineering of microbial strains for increased productivity and substrate utilisation.

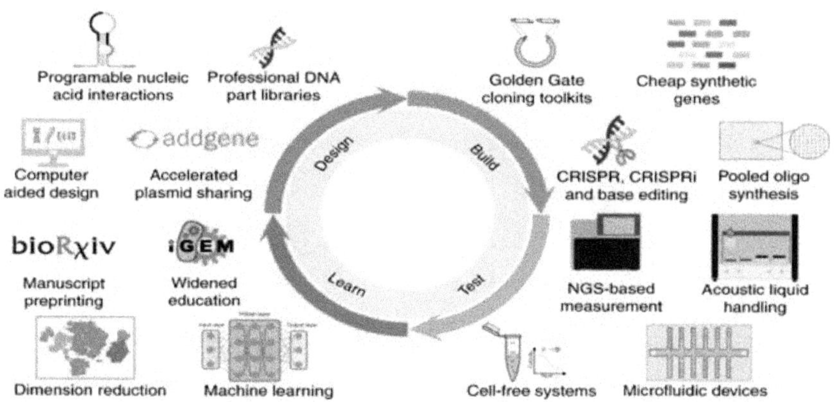

2. Metabolic Engineering:

Through the use of metabolic engineering techniques, it is possible to optimise cellular metabolism and increase the yield of desired substances. To improve target product yields and titers, this entails altering metabolic pathways, enzyme kinetics, and regulatory components within microbial hosts.

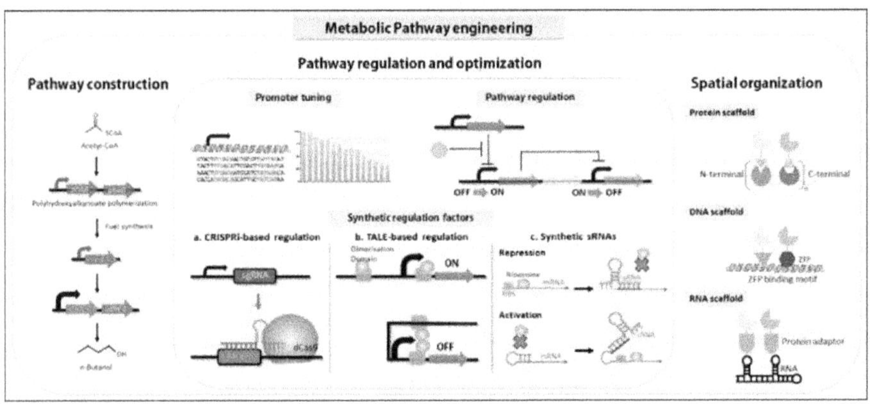

3. High-Throughput Screening:

High-throughput screening techniques make it easier to quickly test and characterise enzymes, fermentation conditions, and microbial strains. As a result, the development of biocatalysts and bioprocesses for industrial use is accelerated.

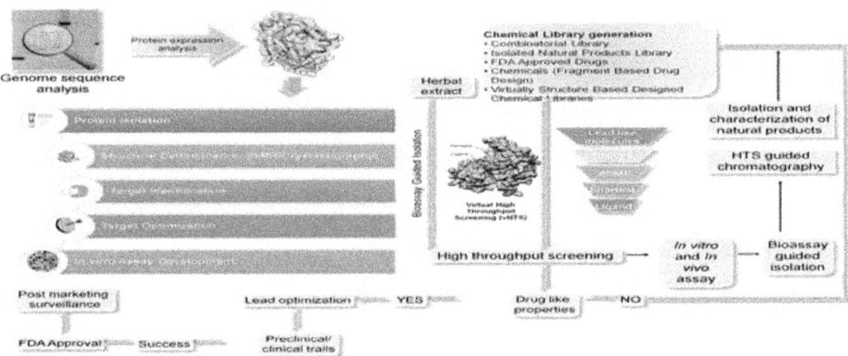

4. Omics Technologies:

Omics technologies offer a thorough understanding of the molecular mechanisms underpinning biological systems. Examples of these technologies include proteomics, metabolomics, and genomics. Systems-level analysis and metabolic pathway optimisation are made possible by the integration of omics data, which leads to enhanced performance.

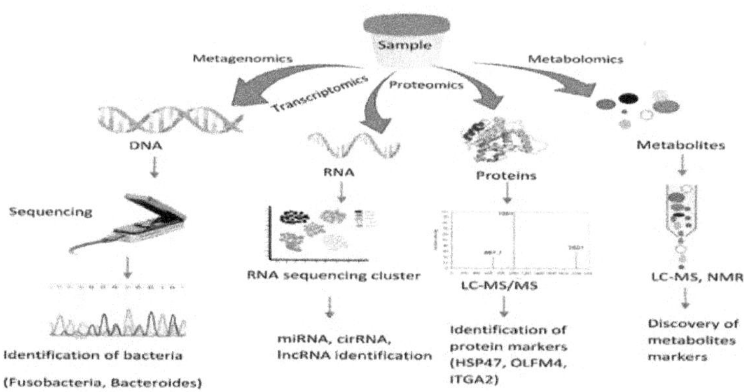

5. Process Intensification:

Strategies for process intensification are designed to make bioprocesses more productive and efficient while using less resources and producing less waste. This covers the creation of integrated biorefinery concepts, immobilised enzyme reactors, and continuous fermentation systems.

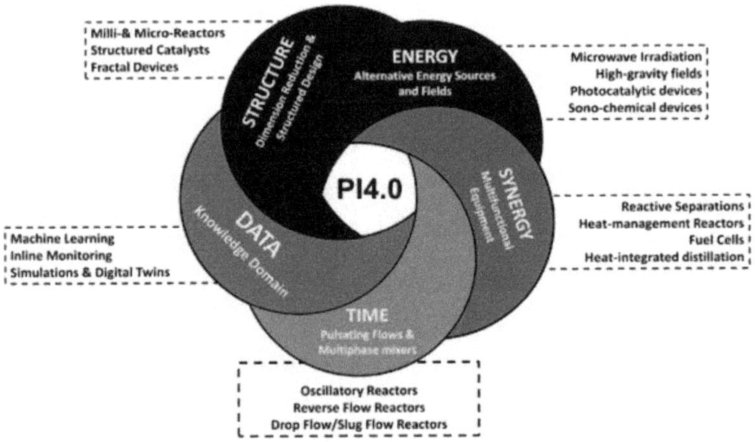

6. Automation and Digitalization:

Process control, monitoring, and optimisation in industrial biotechnology are improved by the integration of digital technologies, such as automation, machine learning (ML), and artificial intelligence (AI). By doing this, operating costs and time-to-market are decreased while process reliability, reproducibility, and scalability are improved.

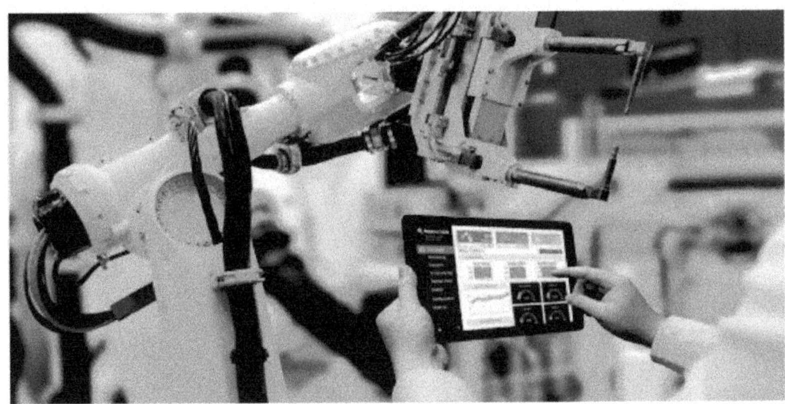

7. Innovative Bioreactor Designs:

The growing of microbial cells under ideal circumstances for optimal productivity and product quality is made possible by innovations in bioreactor design. This involves creating bioreactors that have exact control over variables including mixing, pH, temperature, and oxygen concentrations.

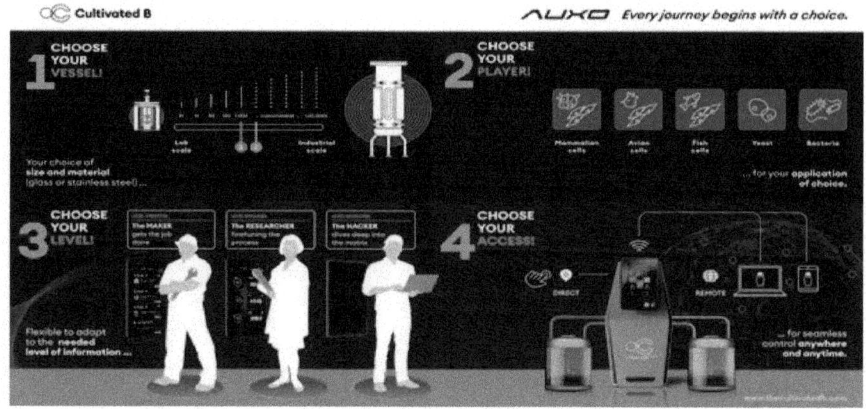

8. Advanced Analytical Techniques:

High-performance liquid chromatography (HPLC), mass spectrometry, and nuclear magnetic resonance (NMR) spectroscopy are examples of advanced analytical techniques that offer comprehensive characterization of bioproducts and process intermediates. This makes optimisation, quality assurance, and process monitoring easier.

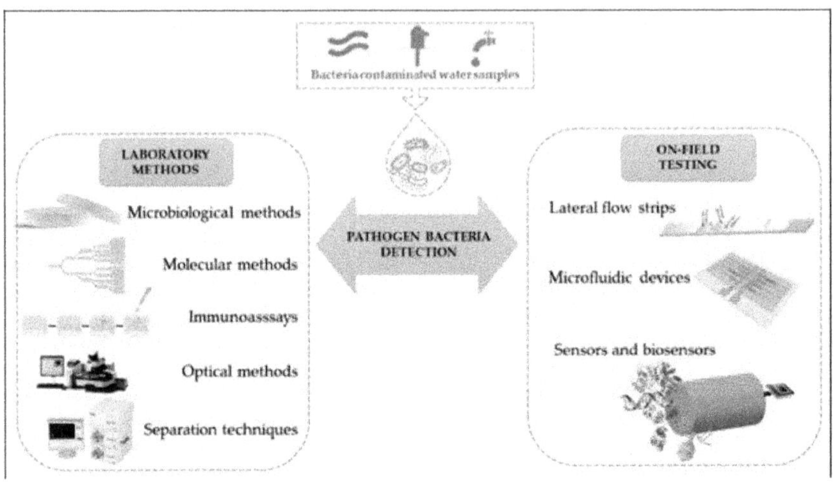

9. Bioprocess Modelling and Simulation:

Predictive analysis of system behaviour and process parameter optimisation are made possible by mathematical modelling and simulation of bioprocesses. This helps to cut the cost and labour of experiments while designing reliable and effective bioprocesses.

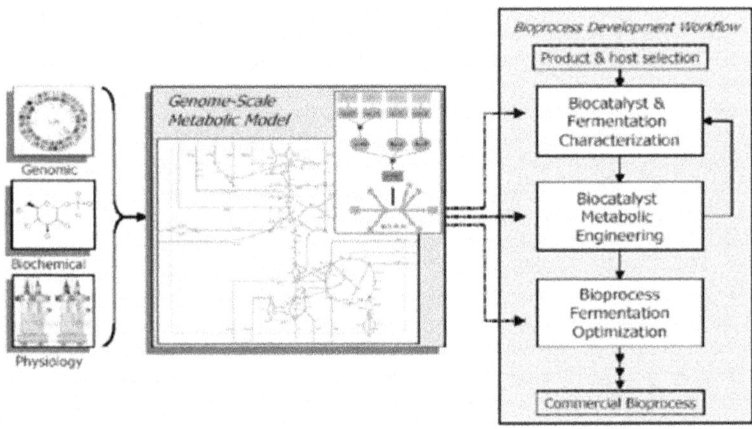

10. Microbiome Engineering:

The goal of microbiome engineering is to improve bioprocess performance and ecosystem functions by modifying microbial communities. This covers the management of microbial consortiums for enhanced bioremediation, biogas generation, and biomass degradation.

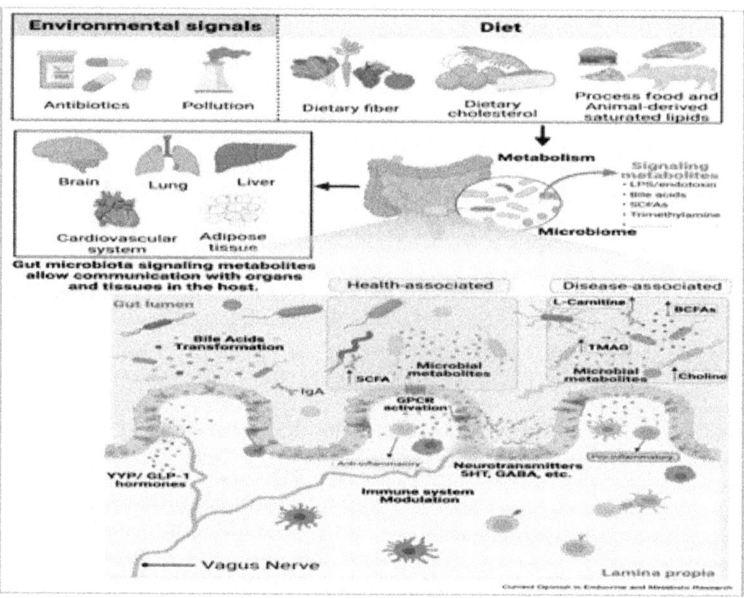

CHALLENGES AND OPPORTUNITIES

Challenges:

1. Economic Viability:

The commercialization of industrial biotechnology processes and products is severely hampered by high upfront capital costs and protracted development schedules.

2. Scale-Up Challenges:

Keeping processes stable, repeatable, and economically viable while expanding bioprocesses from the laboratory to the industrial level poses certain technical difficulties.

3. Regulatory Restraints:

Tight regulations pertaining to product quality, safety, and environmental effect impose burdens on compliance and may cause biotechnology-derived items to enter the market later than expected.

4. Technological Constraints:

Despite progress, a number of technological constraints still prevent bioprocesses from being as productive and efficient as they may be. These constraints include limited enzyme stability, substrate inhibition, and metabolic pathway bottlenecks.

5. Infrastructure Requirements:

Lack of specialised equipment, facilities, and trained labour may be a barrier to the general adoption of industrial biotechnology in some areas. This includes infrastructure for bioprocessing.

Opportunities

1. Sustainable Development:

By lowering greenhouse gas emissions, resource depletion, and environmental degradation, industrial biotechnology presents prospects for the development of sustainable substitutes for fossil fuel-based enterprises.

2. Bio-Based Economy:

Developing new bio-based materials, products, and energy sources from renewable biomass feedstocks is made possible by the shift to a bio-based economy.

3. Biorefinery Concepts:

Various biomass feedstocks can be valued into a variety of high-value products, such as chemicals, materials, medicines, and biofuels. This is made possible by integrated biorefinery concepts.

4. Circular Economy Initiatives:

By facilitating the recycling, reuse, and repurposing of waste streams and byproducts from diverse industries, industrial biotechnology supports circular economy initiatives.

5. Advanced Biocatalysts:

Opportunities to raise the productivity, sustainability, and selectivity of bioprocesses exist through ongoing study and development of novel biocatalysts, enzymes, and microbial strains with improved characteristics.

6. Digitalization and Automation:

The industrial biotechnology sector benefits from the integration of digital technologies, including automation, artificial intelligence (AI), and big data analytics, since they improve process control, optimization, and decision-making.

7. Partnerships and Cooperation:

Working together, the public, private, and academic sectors promote innovation, technology transfer, and knowledge sharing, which speeds up the creation and marketability of industrial biotechnology solutions.

8. Consumer Awareness:

Growing consumer awareness and the need for environmentally friendly and sustainable products open up new markets for bio-based substitutes in a number of industries, such as food, cosmetics, packaging, and textiles.

FUTURE DIRECTIONS:

1. Projects For The Circular Economy:

By keeping a close eye on these projects, integrated biorefinery models will be developed, allowing a variety of biomass feedstocks to be valued into a range of high-value products while producing the least amount of trash possible.

2. Bio-Based Value Chains:

As bio-based products replace traditional fossil-based alternatives in a variety of industries, the development of bio-based value chains will aid in the shift towards a more resilient and sustainable economy.

3. Advanced Biosimilars and Biologics:

New developments in biosimilars and biologics, such as gene therapies, cell therapies, and next-generation monoclonal antibodies, will increase the number of treatments available for complex illnesses and personalised medicine.

4. Novel Drug Delivery Systems:

By permitting targeted delivery and controlled release of therapeutic agents, the development of novel drug delivery systems, such as hydrogels, liposomes, and nanoparticles, will improve the safety, efficacy, and specificity of biopharmaceuticals.

5. Biomanufacturing Innovation:

Technological innovations in biomanufacturing, such as continuous processing, modular manufacturing platforms, and single-use systems, will lower costs and have a positive environmental impact while enhancing process flexibility, efficiency, and scalability.

6. Integration of Digital Technologies:

By enabling predictive modelling, real-time monitoring, and bioprocess optimisation, the integration of digital technologies—such as automation, machine learning, and artificial intelligence (AI)—will speed up development times and enhance product quality.

7. Personalised Medicine:

New advances in proteomics, genomics, and biomarker identification will open the door to personalised medicine strategies that customise treatment plans based on the genetic composition, illness characteristics, and therapeutic responses of individual patients.

8. Bioinformatics and Systems Biology:

By combining omics, systems biology, and bioinformatics technology, it will be possible to analyse and simulate biological systems in great detail. This will provide light on intricate metabolic pathways and cellular functions, allowing for more precise manipulation and optimisation.

9. Global Cooperation and Regulation:

Technology transfer, information exchange, and market access for industrial biotechnology solutions will be facilitated by increased global collaboration and harmonisation of regulatory frameworks, which will promote innovation and sustainable development globally.

CONCLUSION

Industrial biotechnology is a bright thread that connects innovation, sustainability, and economic prosperity in the great scheme of human progress. This groundbreaking field holds the key to opening doors to a future where products are more sustainably produced, processes are greener, and perspectives are altered by the limitless potential of life. It can be applied to anything from the fermenters of biorefineries to the synthetic biology labs.

Beyond conventional limits, industrial biotechnology has penetrated various industries and provided creative answers to some of the most important problems facing society. It has released the creative potential of nature to revolutionise manufacturing, agriculture, healthcare, and environmental stewardship through the combination of biology, chemistry, and engineering.

We are reminded of the tremendous advancements achieved thus far and the enormous prospects that await us when we consider our journey through the domains of industrial biotechnology. A more sustainable and resilient future is made possible by the promise of improved biomanufacturing technologies, bio-based value chains, and circular economy efforts.

But there are still obstacles to overcome, such as financial impediments, legal restrictions, and technical limitations, which call for our combined creativity and perseverance. We can meet these challenges and fully utilise industrial biotechnology to create a world where prosperity coexists with the environment and human endeavours are thoughtfully and sustainably cultivated. We can do this by embracing collaboration, innovation, and responsible stewardship.

Let us carry forward the lessons learned, the insights gained, and the vision of a future where processes are transformed, products are elevated, and perspectives are enlightened by the transformative power of industrial biotechnology as we bid farewell to this exploration of industrial biotechnology. Let's set out on a journey together to a better future where biotechnology's promise is fulfilled for the good of humanity.

REFERENCES

1. Chisti, Y. (2018). Industrial biotechnology trends and opportunities. Trends in biotechnology, 36(2), 198-201.
2. Nielsen, J., & Keasling, J. D. (2016). Engineering cellular metabolism. Cell, 164(6), 1185-1197.
3. Lee, S. Y., Kim, H. U., & Chae, T. U. (2019). Recent advances in systems metabolic engineering tools and strategies. Current opinion in biotechnology, 57, 182-190.
4. Piddock, L. J., & Hall, A. R. (2020). Antibiotic resistance in the context of the COVID-19 pandemic: a review. Journal of antimicrobial chemotherapy, 75(11), 3419-3420.
5. Stephanopoulos, G., & Nielsen, J. (2019). Industrial biotechnology: tools and applications. Metabolic engineering, 56, 2-10.
6. Wittmann, C., & Liao, J. C. (2017). Bio-based production of chemicals, materials and fuels—Corynebacterium glutamicum as versatile cell factory. Current opinion in biotechnology, 45, 162-169.
7. Kumar, V., & Park, S. (2018). Potential and limitations of Klebsiella pneumoniae as a microbial cell factory utilizing glycerol as the carbon source. Biotechnology advances, 36(6), 1505-1521.
8. Zabed, H., Sahu, J. N., Boyce, A. N., Faruq, G., & Hossain, M. S. (2017). Bioethanol production from renewable sources: current perspectives and technological progress. Renewables: Wind, Water, and Solar, 4(1), 2.
9. Glick, B. R. (2017). Metabolic load and heterologous gene expression. Biotechnology advances, 35(2), 177-188.
10. Kumar, V., & Park, S. (2019). Potential and limitations of Klebsiella pneumoniae as a microbial cell factory utilizing glycerol as the carbon source. Biotechnology advances, 36(6), 1505-1521.

CHAPTER FIVE

HARVESTING INNOVATIONS: AGRICULTURAL BIOTECHNOLOGY

INTRODUCTION TO AGRICULTURAL BIOTECHNOLOGY: -

A wide range of scientific methods and approaches that use biological systems to increase agricultural production, sustainability, and food security are together referred to as agricultural biotechnology. The importance of agricultural biotechnology in contemporary agriculture cannot be emphasized. It is an effective instrument for tackling some of the most important issues pertaining to sustainability and global food production. Researchers and farmers alike may create crops and livestock with enhanced characteristics, resilience, and nutritional value by utilizing the concepts of biotechnology. Agricultural biotechnology is essentially the use of molecular biology, genetic engineering, and other cutting-edge technologies to improve animals, crops, and farming methods.

To fulfil the increasing demands of a world population that is rising at a rapid pace, one of the main objectives of agricultural biotechnology is to boost crop yields. Scientists can improve features like disease resistance, drought tolerance, and environmental adaptability to increase agricultural output using genetic editing and breeding methods. To ensure food security in areas susceptible to food shortages and agricultural instability, this enhanced production potential is essential. Additionally, agricultural biotechnology is essential in raising the nutritional value of crops, which helps to alleviate diet-related health problems and malnutrition. Scientists can increase the amounts of vital nutrients, vitamins, and minerals in staple crops using methods like bio-fortification, making the crops more nutrient-dense and advantageous for human consumption. This might help fight the widespread micronutrient deficits and hidden hunger that exist throughout the world.

Aside from nutrition and productivity, agricultural biotechnology plays a major role in managing pests and diseases in agriculture. Farmers can limit crop losses due to insect infestations and illnesses and lessen their need on chemical pesticides by introducing genetic characteristics that give resistance to pests and pathogens. This reduces the hazards of pesticide usage to human health and the environment, while also encouraging sustainable agricultural methods. All things considered, agricultural biotechnology is a potent instrument for furthering the objectives of contemporary agriculture, ranging from boosting resilience and production to enhancing sustainability and nutrition. In order to handle the difficult issues of feeding a growing global population while minimizing the environmental imprint of agricultural operations, it is imperative that innovation and acceptance in this area continue. With every step we take in the field of biotechnology, there is still hope for revolutionary advances in agriculture and a more sustainable and food-secure future for future generations.

HISTORICAL BACKGROUND OF AGRICULTURAL BIOTECHNOLOGY: -

A fascinating journey characterized by important turning points and ground-breaking discoveries that have influenced modern agriculture is the history of agricultural biotechnology. Although the area of biotechnology in agriculture has its origins in antiquated methods like fermentation and selective breeding, it was not until the 20th century that new scientific disciplines and technological advancements gave rise to the subject as we know today.

Early Agricultural Innovations: Crop domestication, hybridization, and fermentation are examples of early agricultural innovations practiced by ancient civilizations including the Sumerians, Egyptians, and Chinese. These prehistoric farming methods served as the model for contemporary breeding procedures.

DNA discovery: James Watson and Francis Crick's 1953 discovery of the DNA structure was a turning point in the development of biotechnology. This discovery cleared the path for developments in molecular biology and genetic engineering while also giving scientists a better knowledge of the genetic code.

Creation of Recombinant DNA Technology: In the 1970s, researchers created a technique known as recombinant DNA that made it possible for them to modify and transfer genes across other creatures. This discovery created new avenues for the manipulation of DNA and the development of genetically modified organisms, such as crops with desired characteristics.

Introduction of Transgenic Crops: In 1983, scientists successfully introduced a bacterial gene into tobacco plants to create the first transgenic plant, proving that genetic manipulation of plants was feasible. The creation of genetically modified (GM) crops with characteristics like insect resistance, herbicide tolerance, and increased yield was made possible by this.

GM Crop Commercialization: The first genetically modified (GM) crops were commercially released in the 1990s. These included insect-resistant cotton and maize, as well as soybeans that could withstand herbicides. These crops gave farmers new techniques for controlling weeds and pests, which raised output and decreased the need for chemical inputs.

Developments in Gene Editing and Genomic Analysis: The Human Genome Project's completion in 2003 and the CRISPR-Cas9 gene editing technique's introduction in the 2010s completely changed the biotechnology industry. Thanks to these developments, it is now possible to precisely modify the genomes of plants and animals, creating new opportunities for crop enhancement and trait modification.

Growth of Biotechnological Applications: Agricultural biotechnology has broadened beyond crop biotechnology to encompass a variety of uses, including the creation of genetically modified animals, microbial bio-fertilizers, and bioremediation methods for managing soil and water.

Public Debate and Regulatory problems: As genetically modified (GM) crops have become widely used, there has been public discussion and regulatory problems pertaining to safety, environmental effect, and ethical issues. Different regulatory frameworks have been put in place by governments worldwide to control the application of biotechnology in agriculture while striking a balance between risk assessment, public safety, and innovation.

New Developments and Prospects: In the future, developments in synthetic biology, precision breeding, and data-driven farming techniques will propel agricultural biotechnology forward. Precision farming and digital farming are two examples of agricultural technologies that might be integrated with biotechnology to improve productivity, sustainability, and resistance to climate change and other global concerns.

In conclusion, agricultural biotechnology's history is a monument to scientific creativity and human ingenuity, with each significant development building on the successes of the previous period to usher agriculture into a new one full of promise and opportunity. The future of agriculture looks brighter and more sustainable than ever as we continue to solve the mysteries of the genome and leverage the power of biotechnology.

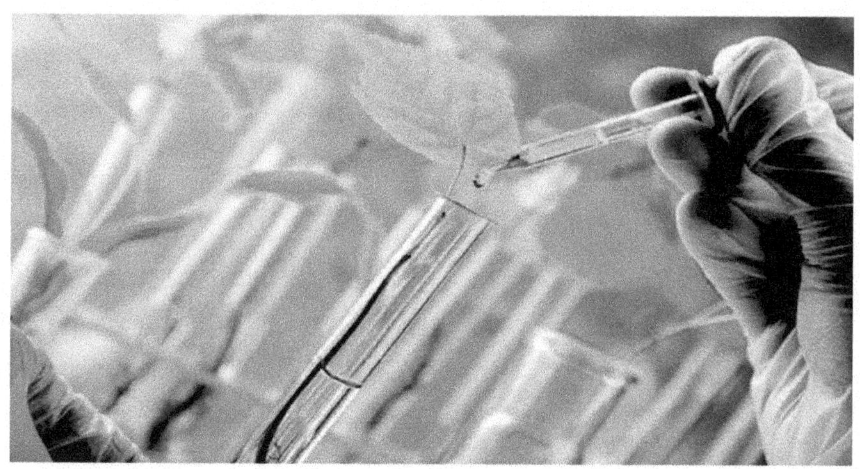

GENETIC ENGINEERING TECHNIQUES IN AGRICULTURAL BIOTECHNOLOGY: -

Agricultural biotechnology relies heavily on genetic engineering techniques because they provide effective means of changing the genetic composition of crops and livestock to enhance their resilience, production, and characteristics. In agricultural biotechnology, the following are some essential genetic engineering techniques:

Gene Editing (e.g., CRISPR-Cas9):

- Gene editing (such as CRISPR-Cas9): CRISPR-Cas9, or Clustered Regularly Interspaced Short Palindromic Repeats-CRISPR associated protein 9, is a cutting-edge method for precise genome-wide DNA sequence change.

- The mechanism of CRISPR-Cas9 involves directing the Cas9 enzyme to a particular target DNA sequence so that it may cut the DNA there.

- The DNA sequence can then alter as a result of the cell's own repair mechanisms healing these breaks.
- CRISPR-Cas9 is used in agriculture to modify certain features without introducing foreign DNA by introducing targeted mutations or edits in the genome of crops or livestock.

- CRISPR-Cas9 is a useful tool for crop improvement and trait modification because of its benefits, which include high precision, efficiency, and adaptability.

Genetic alteration:

- Creating genetically modified organisms (GMOs) with desired properties is achieved by introducing foreign genes, or transgenes, from one species into the genome of another.
- An example of genetic alteration is the creation of transgenic crops.
- Isolating the desired gene, putting it onto a vector (like a plasmid), and then introducing the vector into the target plant cells using methods like Agrobacterium-mediated transformation or biolistic are the usual steps involved in producing transgenic crops.
- In agriculture, transgenic crops have gained widespread acceptance because they provide advantages including higher yields, lower chemical input requirements, and improved insect control.
- **Marker-Assisted Breeding:**
- Molecular markers, like as DNA sequences or genetic markers, are used in marker-assisted breeding, a technique that helps pick desired features in traditional breeding programs.
- Molecular markers are distinct DNA sequences linked to certain characteristics of interest, including prospective yield or resistance to illness.

- Through the examination of genetic markers found in various plant types or breeding lines, breeders may more correctly and effectively identify individuals with desirable features.

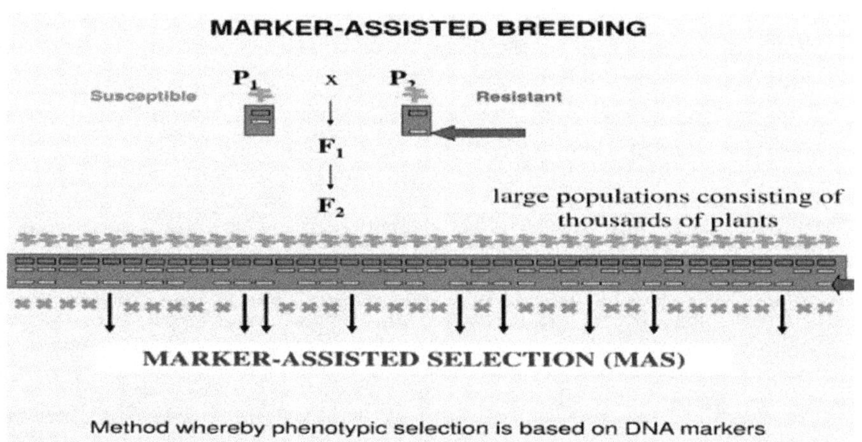

- **APPLICATIONS OF AGRICULTURAL BIOTECHNOLOGY: -**

  A vast range of applications aiming at boosting animal farming methods and crop production, sustainability, and nutritional quality are included in agricultural biotechnology.

  The following are some important uses for agricultural biotechnology:

Creation of Genetically Modified (GM) Crops: To overcome obstacles in agriculture and boost resilience and production, GM crops have been created with a range of features.

Herbicide tolerance: Farmers can more successfully manage weeds while limiting crop damage thanks to genetically modified crops that are developed to withstand particular herbicides.

Insect resistance: By expressing proteins poisonous to particular insect pests, genetically modified crops might lessen agricultural losses brought on by pest damage and the need for chemical-pesticides.

Drought tolerance: By genetically modifying crops, it is possible to make them resistant to dry spells, allowing for their cultivation in desert environments.

Enhancement of Crop nutritious Content by Bio-fortification: In order to combat hunger and promote human health, bio fortification entails raising the nutritious content of crops.

Crops can be bio fortified to produce larger concentrations of important nutrients by introducing genes involved in the synthesis of critical nutrients including vitamins, minerals, and amino acids

.

For instance, communities that depend on rice as a main meal may be able to reduce their risk of vitamin A insufficiency thanks to bio fortified crops like golden rice, which is designed to generate beta-carotene, a precursor of vitamin A.

Improving Crop Yield and Productivity using Precision Breeding Methods:

Utilizing cutting-edge breeding technology and genetic data, precision breeding methods hasten the creation of superior-crop-varieties. Breeders can select for favourable features at the molecular level by recognizing them.

- **BIOTECHNOLOGY IN LIVESTOCK FARMING: -**

Biotechnology provides a variety of instruments and methods in livestock production with the goal of enhancing animal well-being, productivity, and health. An examination of the use of biotechnology in this situation is as below:

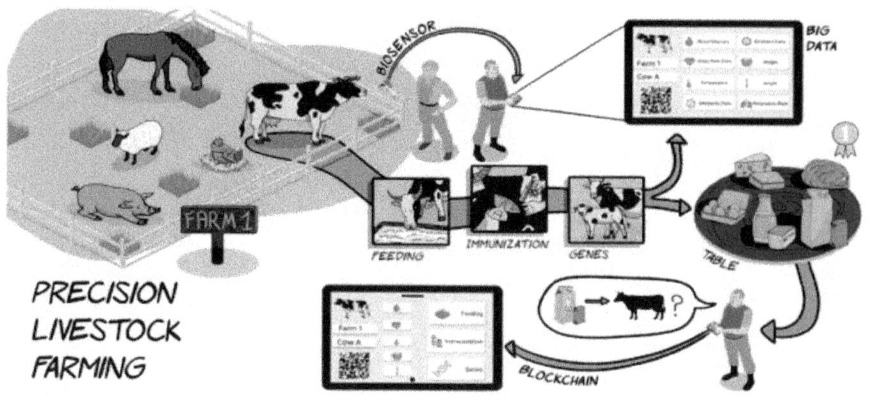

Enter Caption

Genetically Modified Animals: Thanks to biotechnology, it is possible to create animals that have specific genetic modifications. For example, scientists have genetically modified animals to produce more milk or meat, develop faster, and use less feed. These animals are frequently genetically altered to express particular genes linked to metabolic processes or growth hormones.

Disease Resistance: The development of cattle with heightened disease resistance is greatly aided by biotechnology. Animal genomes can have genes linked to disease resistance added through genetic engineering. This can aid in the fight against infectious illnesses that seriously compromise the health and productivity of cattle.

Better Nutrition: Through a variety of techniques, biotechnology makes it possible to improve the nutrition of animals. For instance, scientists can increase the amount of protein or key amino acids in crops used to make animal feed by genetically modifying such crops. Furthermore, genetically engineered microbes that generate enzymes or other additives to improve livestock's digestion and absorption of nutrients are made possible by biotechnology.

Reproductive Biotechnologies: By using cutting-edge reproductive methods, biotechnology can increase cattle genetic selection and breeding efficiency. This covers techniques such as cloning, in vitro fertilization, embryo transfer, and artificial insemination. Farmers may expedite genetic improvement initiatives within their herds and transmit better genetic features using these strategies.

Health Monitoring and Management: Tools for tracking and maintaining the wellbeing and health of animals are made possible by biotechnology. Molecular diagnostic tools facilitate the prompt and precise identification of pathogens, hence enabling early illness diagnosis and action. Furthermore, biotechnological methods like gene editing show promise in creating animal models of human diseases, which will aid in medical research and the creation of new drugs.

Environmental Sustainability: By lessening the environmental impact of animal agriculture, biotechnology helps to promote environmental sustainability in livestock production. For instance, animals that have undergone genetic engineering and gained greater feed efficiency generate less waste and greenhouse gas emissions per unit of production. Furthermore, biotechnology advancements in waste management, such the use of microbes to decompose animal faeces and produce biogas or bio-fertilizers, lessen pollution in the environment.

Social and Ethical Issues: The use of biotechnology in cattle production brings up social and ethical issues pertaining to consumer acceptability, human health, and animal welfare. Transparent communication, ethical principles, and regulatory monitoring are crucial in addressing these issues and guaranteeing that biotechnology breakthroughs in animal production are in accordance with community values and expectations.

- **ENVIRONMENTAL APPLICATIONS: -**

  Through a variety of uses, agricultural biotechnology holds enormous promise for tackling environmental issues and increasing sustainability. It can support sustainability and environmental protection in the following ways:

Bio-fertilizers are microbial-based products that include beneficial bacteria, fungus, or other microorganisms that improve soil fertility and nutrient availability. Their development and manufacturing are made possible by agricultural biotechnology. By fixing atmospheric nitrogen, solubilizing phosphorus, and fostering plant development, these bio-fertilizers can lessen the need for artificial chemical fertilizers. Bio-fertilizers lessen environmental contamination brought on by nutrient runoff and leaching and promote sustainable agriculture practices by enhancing soil health and nutrient cycling.

Innovative bioremediation techniques are made possible by biotechnology and may be used to clean up polluted soils, water bodies, and ecosystems. Bioengineered microorganisms have the ability to break down many contaminants, including industrial chemicals, pesticides, hydrocarbons, and heavy metals, into less toxic or hazardous forms. Bioremediation methods provide an economical and ecologically sustainable means of repairing damaged habitats and reducing the negative effects of pollution on ecosystems and public health.

Using a technique known as phytoremediation, agricultural biotechnology can take use of plants' innate capacity to eliminate pollutants from the environment. Using biotechnological techniques, phytoremediation may be made more efficient and successful by creating plants with better capacities for detoxifying, up-taking, and transporting pollutants. These genetically engineered plants provide a long-term, environmentally beneficial way to clean up polluted groundwater, wastewater, and soil.

Developing carbon sequestration plans to slow down global warming is greatly aided by agricultural biotechnology. Through photosynthesis, genetically modified crops with improved carbon capture and storage capabilities may absorb more carbon dioxide from the atmosphere and store it in organic matter in the soil. Furthermore, biotechnology makes it easier to create perennial grasses with deep root systems and bioenergy crops, both of which help to trap carbon in the soil. These carbon sequestration techniques support attempts to mitigate climate change by offsetting greenhouse gas emissions from agricultural operations.

By lowering the need for chemical pesticides in agriculture, biotechnology helps to preserve the environment. Because genetically modified crops have inherent insect resistance, less pesticide is needed to be applied, which lowers the amount of pesticide residues in the environment and lowers the possibility that non-target creatures may suffer ecological damage. This guarantees sustainable pest management techniques in agriculture while promoting biodiversity conservation and ecosystem health.

- **FUTURE PERSPECTIVES: -**

Precision Agriculture and Digital Farming: Precision agriculture and digital farming techniques will transform agriculture via the merging of biotechnology, artificial intelligence (AI), and big data analytics. In order to optimize crop management practices, such as irrigation scheduling, fertilizer application, and pest control, AI-powered algorithms will analyze enormous amounts of data from sensors, drones, satellites, and IoT devices. This will lead to increased yields, resource efficiency, and environmental sustainability.

Precision breeding and genomics: New developments in genome editing, genomics, and marker-assisted breeding may hasten the creation of better characteristics in crops and livestock, such as increased yields, greater nutritional value, and resistance to biotic and abiotic challenges. A quicker and more accurate genetic improvement in agricultural species will result from the precise and targeted alterations of plant and animal genomes made possible by precision breeding techniques, such as CRISPR-Cas9 and other gene editing technologies.

Synthetic biology:- Synthetic biology techniques will make it possible to build and engineer biological systems for particular agricultural purposes, such as the production of high-value compounds, biofuels, and bioplastics from renewable feed stocks. Synthetic biology is closely related to metabolic engineering. In order to optimize productivity, resource usage, and environmental sustainability in microbial and plant systems, metabolic engineering approaches will be utilized. This will open the door for the development of bio-based substitutes for traditional agricultural inputs and products.

Nanotechnology and Smart Materials: By offering cutting-edge methods for managing soil health, delivering nutrients, and protecting crops, nanotechnology will have a big impact on agriculture. Targeted pesticide delivery, controlled fertilizer release, and soil and plant health parameter monitoring will all be made possible by nano-materials and smart nano-devices, which will result in more effective and sustainable farming methods with lower environmental impact.

Sustainable Agro-ecosystems and Climate-Resilient Crops: Biotechnology will help create climate-resilient agro-ecosystems and crops that can endure the effects of climate change, including harsh weather, drought, heat stress, and insect outbreaks. To increase agricultural resilience and adaptability to changing climatic circumstances, breeding programs will concentrate on choosing and breeding crops with characteristics for better heat and drought tolerance, disease resistance, and carbon sequestration capability.

Vertical farming and controlled environment agriculture (CEA): With the use of biotechnology, these two practices—where crops are cultivated indoors with ideal environmental conditions—will become more widespread. Fresh fruits, vegetables, and herbs can be produced year-round in urban areas using genetically modified crops with features for improved growth, yield, and quality under artificial lighting and hydroponic or aeroponic cultivation systems. This will lessen the environmental impact of food production and increase food security in areas with high population densities.

All things considered, agricultural biotechnology has a lot of potential to address global issues, change the food production process, and advance environmental sustainability, resilience, and fairness in agricultural systems all over the world. To guarantee the appropriate and fair use of biotechnological discoveries for the benefit of society and the environment, it is imperative to take into account the ethical, social, and regulatory consequences of these advancements.

- **CHALLENGES AND LIMITATIONS: -**

There is a lot of promise in agricultural biotechnology to solve problems related to food production, sustainability, and environmental preservation. To fully reap its benefits, though, a number of obstacles and restrictions must be overcome. The following are some of the main obstacles that agricultural biotechnology faces:

Regulatory Obstacles: In many nations, agricultural biotechnology products—particularly genetically modified organisms (GMOs)—are governed by strict regulatory systems. The introduction of biotech crops and inventions into the market can be delayed by the protracted, costly, and intricate regulatory approval procedure. For biotech goods to be adopted and traded globally, regulatory requirements across nations and regions must be harmonized.

Public Perception and Acceptance: Because of worries about food safety, environmental dangers, and ethical issues, certain members of the public frequently view agricultural biotechnology with suspicion, fear, and rejection. Clear communication, thorough risk assessment, and interaction with stakeholders—consumers, farmers, scientists, legislators, and civil society organizations—are necessary to address public views and foster trust.

Issues with Biodiversity: Concerns over transgenic crops' possible effects on biodiversity are raised by their widespread use, including insect- and herbicide-resistant kinds. Particularly in environmentally sensitive locations and agro-ecosystems with high biodiversity, it is imperative to evaluate and reduce the risks of gene flow, weed resistance, and unexpected ecological repercussions connected with the production of transgenic crops.

Implications for Ethics and Socioeconomics: The application of biotechnology in agriculture brings up issues of justice, equality, and power relations on an ethical and socioeconomic level. It is necessary to address issues like farmer reliance on proprietary technologies, corporate concentration in the seed and agrochemical industries, and socioeconomic disparities in access to the risks and benefits of biotechnology through inclusive governance mechanisms and policies that support social justice and equitable benefit distribution.

Long-term Sustainability and Resilience: Although biotechnology provides temporary boosts to agricultural production and resilience, its ecological effects and long-term sustainability need close observation and control. To evaluate the environmental, social, and economic effects of biotech adoption and guarantee the long-term sustainability and resilience of agricultural systems, ongoing research, monitoring, and adaptive management techniques are required.

- **CONCLUSION: -**

Finally, it should be noted that agricultural biotechnology has great potential to solve both present and future agricultural and environmental issues, such as the loss of biodiversity, climate change, rising food demand, and environmental degradation. We have looked at a variety of agricultural biotechnology applications in this chapter, from crop enhancement and animal farming to environmental remediation and sustainability.

Important topics covered include:

The use of biotechnological instruments and methods for raising animals, improving crops, and protecting the environment.

The creation of genetically modified crops and animals that are more productive, resistant to illness, and have higher nutritional value.

The potential of biotechnology to support environmentally friendly agricultural methods include lowering pesticide usage, enhancing soil health, and saving water.

The application of cutting-edge technologies to address global issues and progress agricultural biotechnology, such as artificial intelligence, nanotechnology, and synthetic biology.

How important it is to address ethical, legal, and socioeconomic issues surrounding agricultural biotechnology, such as public opinion, IP rights, and fair access to innovation.

How important it is to address ethical, legal, and socioeconomic issues surrounding agricultural biotechnology, such as public opinion, IP rights, and fair access to innovation.

The safe, moral, and sustainable application of biotechnological advancements in agriculture requires multidisciplinary cooperation, stakeholder involvement, and responsible stewardship.

Agricultural biotechnology clearly has the power to transform food production, increase environmental sustainability, and raise farmers' and communities' standard of living everywhere. But to fully realize this promise, further investigation, creativity, and conscientious care are needed.

Prioritizing funding for agricultural biotechnology research and development is crucial as we move forward. We also need to encourage cooperation and knowledge sharing among various stakeholders and make sure that the application of biotechnological innovations is done in a way that upholds moral standards, protects the environment, and advances social justice.

Through a combination of innovation, discourse, and a comprehensive approach to agricultural biotechnology, we can harness its revolutionary potential to build a food system that is more resilient, egalitarian, and sustainable for future generations.

- **REFERENCES: -**

- Pingali, P. L. Green revolution: impacts, limits, and the path ahead. *Proc. Natl Acad. Sci. USA* **109**, 12302–12308 (2012).
- Hunter, M. C., Smith, R. G., Schipanski, M. E., Atwood, L. W. & Mortensen, D. A. Agriculture in 2050: recalibrating targets for sustainable intensification. *Bioscience* **67**, 386–391 (2017).
- Hunter, M. C., Smith, R. G., Schipanski, M. E., Atwood, L. W. & Mortensen, D. A. Agriculture in 2050: recalibrating targets for sustainable intensification. *Bioscience* **67**, 386–391 (2017).
- Rosenzweig, C. et al. Assessing agricultural risks of climate change in the 21st century in a global gridded crop model intercomparison. *Proc. Natl Acad. Sci. USA* **111**, 3268–3273 (2014).
- Olsen, K. M. & Wendel, J. F. A bountiful harvest: genomic insights into crop domestication phenotypes. *Annu. Rev. Plant Biol.* **64**, 47–70 (2013).
- Oladosu, Y. et al. Principle and application of plant mutagenesis in crop improvement: a review. *Biotechnol. Biotechnol. Equip.* **30**, 1–16 (2016).
- Friso, G. & Van Wijk, K. J. Posttranslational protein modifications in plant metabolism. *Plant Physiol.* **169**, 1469–1487 (2015).
- Hefferon KL (2015) Nutritionally Enhanced Food Crops; Progress and Perspectives. 3895–3914. 10.3390/ijms16023895.
- Haroon F, Ghazanfar M. Applications of food biotechnology. *J Ecosyst Ecography.* 2016 doi: 10.4172/2157-7625.1000215.
- Crossa, J. et al. Genomic selection in plant breeding: methods, models, and perspectives. *Trends Plant Sci.* **22**, 961–975 (2017).

CHAPTER SIX

ENGINEERING LIFE: EXPLORING SYNTHETIC BIOLOGY

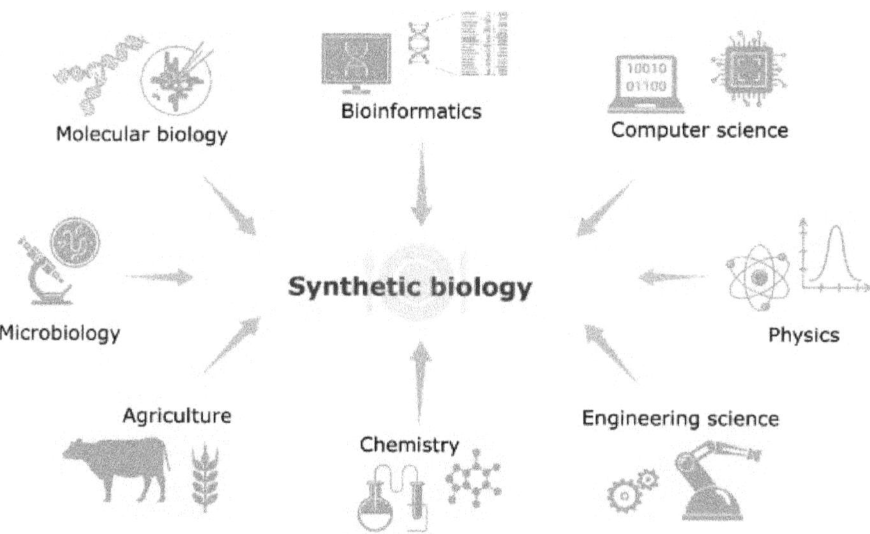

1. INTRODUCTION

Synthetic biology are a multidisciplinary arena that employs machinery, science, and computation to generate artificial biological systems or sections. Synthetic biology (synbio) is a combination of the combination of genetics and biotech. Synthetic biologists design and create biological systems for solving challenges. Synthetic biology is receiving increasing attention from scientists and policymakers in terms of safety, security, ethics, intellectual property, and the possible benefits or drawbacks of this developing area.Synthetic biology aims to copy the emerging abilities of lively systems, such as heredity, genetics, and evolution, using simulated chemical systems. The 1960s discovery of mathematical sense in gene governance, as well as primitive genetic engineering accomplishments in the 1970s, such as recombinant DNA technology, set the way for bionic. In 1961, Francois Jacob and Jacques Monod conducted groundbreaking examination on the lac operon in E. coli, predicting the progress of regulatory networks that ease a cell's result to its environment.

This study laid the foundation for synthetic biology. Barbara Hobom invented the term 'synthetic biology' in 1980 to mention genetically changed microorganisms utilizing recombinant DNA technology. Eric Kool and other presenters presented the term 'synthetic biology' during the 2000 American Chemical Society annual meeting in San Francisco. Craig Venter and his colleagues achieved a significant synthetic biology milestone in 2005 by sequencing the genome of a virus. The obtainability of CRISPR-Cas9 gene editing technology in 2012 revolutionized gene editing, permitting precise and effective modification of DNA sequences. In 2016, scientists synthesized the genome of the eukaryotic cell Saccharomyces cerevisiae, indicating the possibility of constructing complex biological systems.

Synthetic biology explores how to include these guidelines into the process of constructing biological systems. During the latter half of the 1990s, rapid sequencing of DNA and computational techniques made it possible to sequence entire microbial genomes and create a vast library of biological sections and their connections. Synthetic biology has the capacity to address humanity's crucial challenges, including health, agriculture, and environmental sustainability. Nonetheless, it poses ethical, social, and technical challenges. Molecular manipulation raises questions about existence, the confines of human intervention, and responsibility. The complexity of biological systems requires interdisciplinary cooperation and innovation.

Synthetic biology has its roots in the initial stages of genetic modification, when researchers worked with the genetic constitution of an organism, appending or modifying genes to achieve new capabilities. Synthetic biology is characterized by the objective of developing totally new biological systems from scratch using standardized genetic components that act as building blocks. SB can be used in hybrid systems like bioreactors that have mechanical components. Part/plasmid configurations, biochemical/genetic networks languages, build design languages, multiplex computerized genome engineering, RBS design, CRISPR-C liquid-handling technology, and other applications are all possible

Synthetic biology, which includes metabolic engineering, minimum genomes, regulatory circuits, and orthogonal biosystems, has applications in healthcare, industry, and the environment that necessitate continual research for innovation. Figure 1and 2 shows an overview of the synthetic biology discipline[12].

Synthetic biology includes five categories: bioengineering, synthetic genome, protocell synthetic biology, unusual molecular biology, and in silico approaches. The categorizing of synthetic biology starts with a look at strategies for design, which represent several theoretical approaches to manipulating biological systems. Strategies for design can be broadly classified as top-down or bottom-up approaches. Top-down techniques entail changing existing biological systems, generally through manipulation of genes to attain the desired functionality.

Synthetic biology employs a variety of genetic modification tools, including homologous recombination, the The CRISPR- systems, and the synthesis of DNA, to change DNA through diverse mechanisms. Type II CRISPR-Cas systems identify and cleave invading bacteriophages by RNA-directed DNA binding by Cas9. Cas9 nuclease mutations allow RNA-directed binding without DNA cleavage.Cas9's RNA-targeting sequence determines its DNA-binding specificity. Cas9 can target almost every genomic or epigenetic sequence. Engineered biological systems can synthesize therapeutic proteins that target infectious genes, and restore damaged tissues. Agriculture uses synthetic biology to improve crops, manufacture biopesticides, and create GMOs.

In this chapter, we'll explore the captivating world of synthetic biology, including its fundamental rules, cutting-edge applications, and the ethical and societal repercussions of its advancement. Synthetic biology has the potential to transform our environment in fundamental and unprecedented ways, both in the laboratory and on a global level. As we embark on this route of knowledge, let us do so with curiosity, humility, and a strong commitment to responsible stewardship of life.

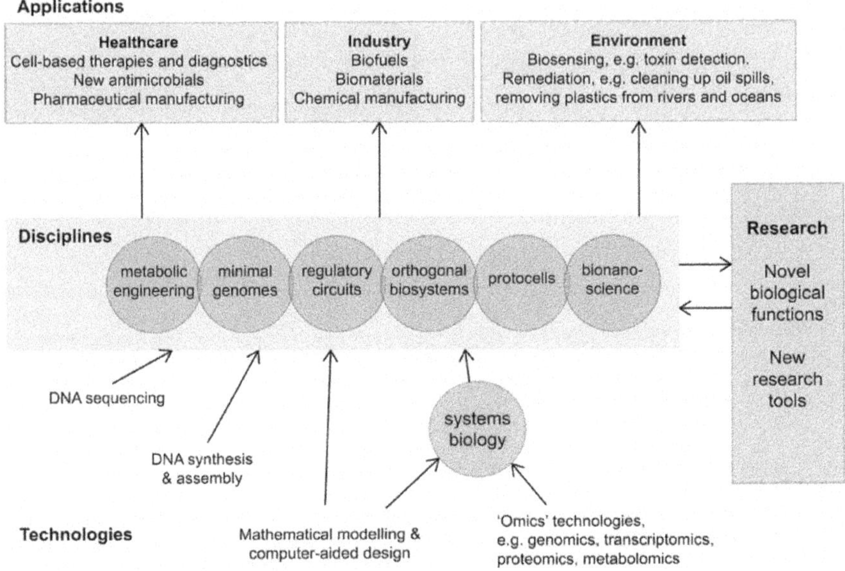

2. Classifications of Synthetic Biology:-

Synthetic biology approaches are used in a variety of areas, including metabolic engineering, minimum genomes, regulatory circuits, and orthogonal biosystems, with continual research necessary to test new ideas and generate new products.There are five categories of synthetic biology that are bioengineering, synthetic genome, protocell synthetic biology, unconventional molecular biology, and in silico techniques (figure 3)[3].

2.1 Bioengineering:-

Bioengineering is the application of engineering knowledge to the fields of medicine and biology. Bioengineers, with extensive engineering knowledge, can work in various fields, including artificial means to assist body functions, such as hearing aids, artificial limbs, and supportive organs. Bioengineering is not synonymous with classical genome engineering, which entails introducing a single gene into an organism. Bioengineers used synthetic biology to develop detailed ideas for altering species and systems of life. This field of synthetic biology has been made possible by continuous developments in DNA-synthesis technology over the years, which now allows for the production of DNA molecules with thousands of base pairs at a competitive cost. The goal is to combine these molecules into whole genomes and transplant them into living cells, effectively replacing the host cell's genome and reprogramming its metabolism to perform new functions.

Bioengineering arose from unique demands, such as doctors' need to bypass the heart, the necessity for replacement organs, being needed for life support systems, and many more. A common example of single-gene genetic engineering is the insertion of the human insulin gene into bacteria to produce transgenic proteins. Bioengineering, a branch of synthetic biology, is the development of entire new signalling pathways that include several genes and regulatory. Further bioengineering is classified into Medical engineering, agriculture engineering, Human factor engineering, genetics, environmental engineering.

2.1.1 Medical Engineering:-

The field of synthetic biology has advanced significantly due to the availability of new biological parts, improved engineering of biological systems, and quicker design cycles enabled by simple nucleic acid synthesis.Medical engineering is the use of engineering principles to medical problems such as organ replacement, instrumentation, and healthcare systems, which may include computer diagnostic applications.

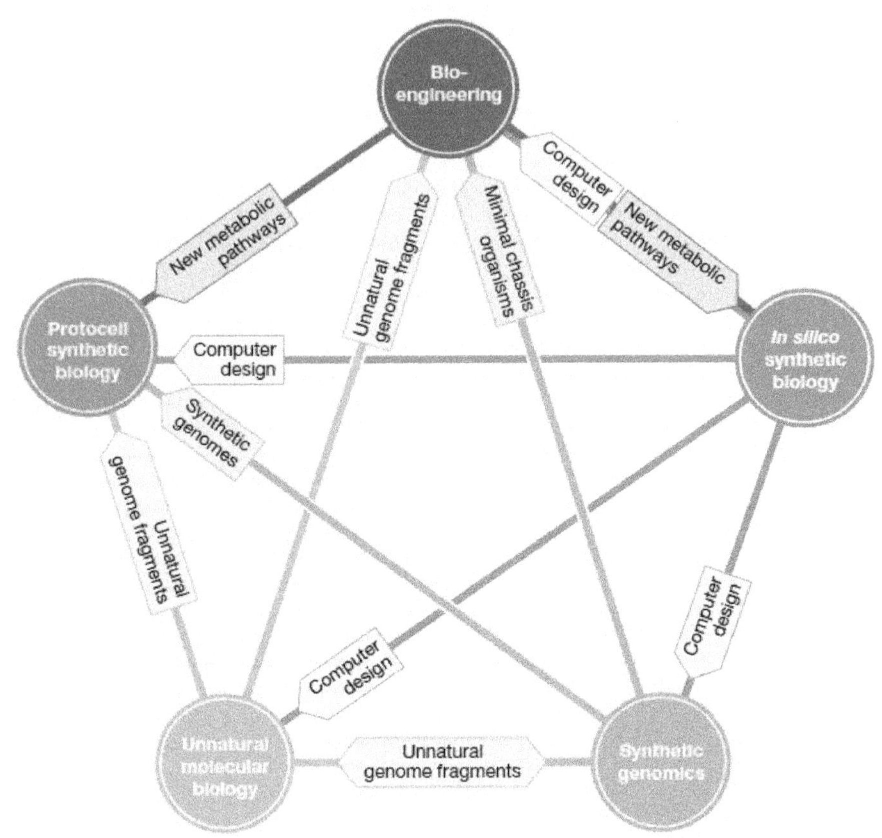

2.1.2 Agriculture Engineering:-

Traditionally, developments in genetic research have helped major sectors such as agriculture, fishery, and forestry. About half of the 1-3% yearly growth in agricultural and livestock productivity to date is thought to have been driven by improved genetics, with rates of genetic gain expected to more than double with the deployment of developing molecular technology.Historical Agricultural Engineering has grown to align with biological engineering, incorporating engineering ideas from diverse disciplines and emphasizing engineering biology, distinguishing it from other physically-based engineering fields.

Plant-based biological engineering for the production is a promising area since agricultural engineers have experience with crop cultivation, agriculture, and controlling pests. This technique can be used to renewable fuels, chemicals, foods, and nutraceuticals, benefiting society by meeting various application needs. Semi-synthetic artemisinin, a strong antimalarial chemical derived from the plant Artemisia annua, was produced in yeast by gradually addressing cytotoxicity and bottlenecks in the biosynthesis route[4]. The modular G-protein coupled receptor (GPCR) system developed using BRET-biosensors can detect a variety of organic compounds, including food spoilage and explosives, by utilizing the odor receptor protein from Caenorhabditis worms.

2.1.3 Enviromental engineering:-

This field, also known as bioenvironmental engineering, is concerned with the application of engineering principles to environmental control in order to protect human health, comfort, and safety. Microbes are exceptional microscopic sensors that can detect, integrate, and dynamically respond to a wide range of environmental variables. Biosensors are genetically modified microorganisms, or standalone biological components, that detect and report on certain environmental variables of interest. Biosensors are an alternative to typical analytical techniques for detecting and quantifying environmental signals because they can convert difficult and/or expensive-to-detect signals of interest into easily detectable results. They can also report on microbial "experiences" at the micron scale in complicated environmental matrices, providing information that would not be available using conventional analytical methods.

2.2 Synthetic genome:-

Synthetic genomics highlights another milestone in synthetic biology: the production of animals with chemically synthesized genomes. Synthetic biology helped advance DNA synthesis techniques, enabling the low-cost production of thousands of base pairs. In January 2008, JCVI scientists Daniel G. Gibson and Hamilton O. Smith successfully built a modified version of the bacteria M. genitalium's genome from scratch. This was substantially different from recombinant DNA research, which involved one-by-one gene alterations, because multiple genes were linked together to produce a new genome. Synthetic genomes begin with single-stranded oligonucleotides and build up from there .Mycoplasma genitalium's genome was the first to be fully chemically synthesized. However, the genome transfer failed to create a viable synthetic M. genitalium strain due to an interruption in the rnpB subunit of RNaseP. The goal is to transfer these compounds into living animal cells, altering the host genome or metabolic pathways for specific activities. In 2010, the same researchers successfully synthesized and transferred the 1.08 Mb Mycoplasma mycoides genome to a close relative.Mycoplasma capricolum. M. mycoides JCVI-syn1.0 is the first synthetic genome-controlled organism. This successful project provided the foundation for creating a basic Mycoplasma organism using JCVI-syn1.0.

Synthesizing oligonucleotides longer than 200 nucleotides with high fidelity remains challenging due to repetitive yield problems caused by imperfect nucleotide chemical purity and damage during synthesis. Even with 99% effectiveness, only 13% of 200-mer molecules will be correct. To create longer DNA sequences, single-stranded oligos are stitched together to form double-stranded DNA fragments. These larger constructs are then assembled to reach genome size. Synthetic DNA may require assembly in a new host to improve efficiency. In these circumstances, genome transplantation technology may be required.

CAD software has been developed to efficiently and consistently design synthetic DNA sequences at the genome size.Synthetic DNA has a vast design space with limitless possibilities, as long as they ensure cell viability and achieve the intended design. While viruses and phages are not considered 'living', they do contain a genome. They can proliferate using a host's resources. Viral genomes range in size from 1759 bps (Porcine circovirus) to 1259 kb (Megavirus chilensis), and can contain either DNA or RNA. In 2002, the polio virus's RNA genome was completely synthesized for the first time. The 7.5 kb cDNA genome was transcribed in vitro using RNA polymerase and may produce infectious virus particles when transferred into a cell-free extract. Recent years have seen the synthesis of viral genomes up to 212 kb in size. Synthesizing and manipulating viral genomes to create libraries has significant potential for therapeutic applications. Rapid development of vaccines and treatments in response to a specific viral variation can help prevent larger epidemics.

2.3 Unantural molecular biology:-

Natural product analogue creation is significant because it provides instruments for chemical biology, allows for the discovery of structure-activity relationships, and gives insight into how natural products interact with their target biomolecules. Analogues are typically required to increase bioavailability and fine-tune chemical action. The 'unnatural molecular biology' method seeks to create fresh forms of life based on a new type of molecular biology, such as new nucleic acids or a different genetic code. Alternative kinds of nucleic acids could be created by modifying distinct DNA or RNA components, such as bases or backbone sugars, to produce new types of nucleotides that can be combined into novel nucleic acids.

2.4 In silico synthetic biology:-

In Silico Biology seeks to enhance understanding of the principles governing the formation of living systems.Different approaches and synthetic biology in silico are interconnected. Creating complex designs, such as metabolic pathways and complete genomes, is a significant challenge for the methods discussed above. As a result, synthetic biology includes a significant in silico branch called system biology, which strives to create computer models for designing biological components and synthetic circuitry to stimulate synthetic creatures. Integrating the five disciplines of synthetic biology into a unified body of study is a logical step. These five tactics focus on various parts of life, such as metabolic regulation, vital ingredients, and biochemical makeup, yet all aim to create novel living creatures. The discipline of synthetic biology employs a variety of methodologies from different approaches, resulting in a broad spectrum of approaches.

As the need for bio-based products and materials grows, automated smart biomanufacturing laboratories are revolutionizing the sector.Historically, metabolic engineering projects were done manually, frequently by trial and error. The first step in automating metabolic pathways is to select chemical targets. External partners, such as consumers interested in commercializing bio-based versions of natural products, pharmaceuticals, or building blocks, often set targets. To produce chemical targets using bio-based methods, viable routes must be identified. It is likely that a natural biosynthetic pathway exists, but it may have been refined by evolution in another host. As a result, even when routes are available, it is typically advantageous to choose enzymes from multiple sources.

A more ambitious effort would be to explore for alternatives to the natural or manmade channels described in the literature. To that goal, retrosynthetic analysis is used. Several computational platforms for retrobiosynthesis exist, including BNICE, GEM-Path RetroPath 2.0, PathPred (36) and Cho et al. Each model has a distinct computational representation of reactions and ranks probable paths differently. Recent research has demonstrated that automated retrosynthetic analysis for synthetic chemistry can outperform expert analysis using cutting-edge machine learning algorithms, including deep learning. Retrosynthetic analysis for biosynthesis, also known as bioretrosynthesis, requires skill in both chemical reactions and enzyme biocatalysis.

2.5 Protocell synthetic biology:-

Synthetic protocells, self-assembled vesicles with a cell-like structure, can replicate biological behaviors including gene expression and enzymatic catalysis. Protocells are artificial entities made up of inanimate components that replicate the structure and some key qualities of a natural cell, and protocell functions are programmed using artificial response networks. The protocell branch of synthetic biology is concerned with the in vitro production of synthetic cells.SPB is a very new research topic that is both connected to and a continuation of various other research fields, hence its boundaries are not well defined. The goal of protocell research is to design, build, and characterize micro-compartmentalized structures that share the unique static and dynamic architecture of primitive or modern living cells. The Ganti chemoton or the Maturana-Varela autopoietic systems have frequently been used as theoretical frameworks for such endeavors.

The most straightforward method for creating a protocell from scratch is to immediately encapsulate naturally occurring genetic circuits such as transcription/translation (TX/TL) within an artificially created vesicle with a continuous membrane structure. Further modifications to the TX/TL system to obtain more controllable computational capability are expected.There have been two fundamental techniques to protocell production. The first class, often known as the top-down strategy, entails creating a minimal cell by decreasing the genome of existing cells. Because many genes are involved in cell-cell communication while others have been shown to be non-essential to cell function, it was previously proposed that genome complexity could be reduced to a minimal set of genes capable of sustaining cell life and reproduction (given external conditions).

3. Approaches used by synthetic biology:-

Formerly synthetic biology has employed four engineering approaches: top down, parallel, orthogonal, and bottom up. Synthetic biologists conduct their research using two strategic approaches: "top-down" and "bottom-up".. Specific genetic components can also be altered or modified to provide the organisms with new features and functions. The ultimate goal is to construct a "minimum genome" or a "minimal cell" (as simple as feasible for life), which may be used as a "chassis" to insert additional genes that change or enrich its biological features and lead to novel activities .

3.1 Top down approach:-

Top-down synthetic biology, in general, exploits aspects of biological systems to build something new. The top-down technique involves re-designing existing organisms (a bacterium or a virus) or gene sequences in order to remove genetic components that are not required for the job that the creature is intended to fulfil.One strategy is to simplify the genome by deleting non-essential genes, reducing the complexity of existing cells. Recent study reveals that the tree of life, which includes eukaryotic and prokaryotic cells, may have originated from a collection of primordial cells instead of a single cell. Eliminating non-essential functions might harm an organism's fitness and result in "fragile" genomes, making the pursuit of the "minimum genome" elusive like the Holy Grail.

3.2 Parallel approach:-

Parallel pathways have been found to be prevalent and pervasive in AG biosynthesis, demonstrating nature's creativity in obtaining different natural products from a small set of genes. Yoon, Sohng, and colleagues discovered that kanamycin A and B are generated in two parallel approach. KanF, a glycosyltransferase in the kan gene cluster, converts NDP-glucose and NDP-N-acetylglucosamine to 2-DOS, which produces 2'-hydroxyparomamine and paromamine. KanE absorbs four distinct pseudodisaccharides as glycosyl acceptors and converts kanamycin B into kanamycin A. The substrate versatility of kanamycin biosynthetic enzymes indicates a high potential for AG combinatorial biosynthesis. Integrating S-4-amino-2-hydroxybutyric acid (AHBA) biosynthetic genes into the kanamycin pathway resulted in the production of amikacin, a semisynthetic AG, and 1-N-AHBA-kanamycin X, a novel AG analogue with increased antibacterial activity.

Parallel pathways in gentamicin biosynthesis:- Gentamicin, a broad-spectrum antibiotic derived from Micromonospora echinospora, consists of five C-series components. It is a potential medication for the treatment of hereditary illnesses as well as a sensitizer for lung cancer cells. The biosynthesis process for gentamicin was first proposed several decades ago, however new research has revised it. Gentamicin A2 is the first pseudotrisaccharide precursor, and it is transformed to gentamicin X2 by several enzymes. Gentamicin G418 and X2 are the initial substrates for two parallel routes that yield gentamicin JI-20A and JI-20B. The exact reaction order and time in gentamicin C1 generation are still unknown due to the presence of many gentamicin congeners and the participation of the epimerase GenB2. Future research may look at the hypothesis that GenB2 is responsible for third parallel pathway and is not essential for gentamicin C biosynthesis.

3.3 Orthogonal approach:-

This strategy, also known as perpendicular engineering or chemical synthetic biology, tries to modify or increase the genetic blueprints of biological things by employing artificial DNA bases or amino acids. This field, related to xenobiology, studies the use of "alien" or xeno chemicals as genetic information carriers, synthesizing compounds similar to DNA canonical bases. By modifying or expanding the genetic code, information beyond the 20 traditional amino Acids can be expressed. Researchers have successfully inserted noncanonical moieties into DNA and proteins, resulting in more diversified biological systems. Directed evolution produces orthogonal enzymes that can incorporate XAAs into proteins and create "mirror life" systems.

3.4 Bottom up approach:-

This approach creates novel biological systems in vitro by assembling 'non-living' biomolecular components, frequently with the goal of building an artificial cell. Bottom-up synthetic biology is an intriguing but challenging method for unraveling the intricacies of biological systems. In this strategy, molecules are assembled in a well-defined form with predictable properties in order to produce a certain biological output. The development of artificial cells has emerged as a significant application over the years. Artificial cells have been imagined as cell-like compartments holding the basic molecules of life that should behave similarly to a real cell in a particular environment.

The "bottom-up" synthetic biology approach creates "protocells" to bridge the gap between non-living and living matter. It consists of three components: a metabolism that extracts energy from the environment, and the system consists of three components: construction blocks (new and old), an informative program (e.g. nucleic acids), and a container for coordination.To do this, three key self-organization concepts are considered: reproduction, replication, and assembly. Reproduction refers to a system's ability to repeat a similar copy of itself, while replication occurs when a system replicates an exact copy of itself, such as the genetic program (DNA) or "software." Assembly happens by the aggregation of vesicles or containers, such as Oparin's coacervates, which contain small droplets of organic molecules such as lipids or liposomes. These structures are membrane-like and contain phospholipids.

4. Application:-

4.1 Production in remote and unconventional areas.:-

Synthetic biology has transformed the manufacture of biochemicals, medicines, and foods using a variety of host species. However, less emphasis has been placed on production technologies for non-laboratory scenarios such as underdeveloped countries, remote military and space missions, and built environment in situ applications. DARPA Battlefield Medicine and NASA's TRISH are two funding efforts that try to solve difficulties and facilitate on-demand manufacturing in these circumstances.

4.2 In Genetic Engineering:-

Engineered mammalian cells for medical applications With the advances in synthetic biology, researchers created various novel therapies using living cell chassis rationally designed. New signaling networks are being developed for many goals, such as producing medicinal biomolecules, creating synthetic gene networks for sensing or diagnostics, and programming.

Adaptable organisms can tolerate disease-related mechanisms and occurrences. This article discusses synthetic biology methodologies for mammalian cell engineering, including metabolic diseases, tissue engineering, cancer treatments, cell therapy, and gene circuit design. Therapies based on CAR-T cells. CARs are designed receptors with both antigen-binding and T cell activation domains. T cells are obtained from patients.

A specific CAR is generated ex vivo and then transferred into the donor patient to kill cancer cells that present the target antigen on their surface.26 CAR-T is a new cell therapy that first emerged in the 2000s. The key advantage of using CAR-based approaches for cancer immunotherapy is that the scFv produced from antibodies has far higher affinities than Conventional TCRs.CARs can target glycolipids, aberrant glycosylated proteins, and conformational variations not identified by TCRs.

SynNotch receptors are artificially created receptors utilized for medical applications. Notch receptors are transmembrane signaling receptors with extracellular, transmembrane, and intracellular domains. SynNotch architects often retain transmembrane and intracellular domains, while the signal-input extracellular domain is designed to detect scFvs and nanobodies, potentially initiating signaling in living cells.

For diabetes. Courbet et al. proposed a technique for detecting aberrant glucose concentrations in human urine samples.They encapsulated the bacterial sensors in hydrogel beads; glucose in urine causes the beads to turn red. The in vitro bacterial glucometer outperformed the detection limit of urinary dipsticks by an order of magnitude.Engineered gut bacteria produce proteins and peptides to cure diabetes. When diabetic rats were given the engineered probiotic L.gasseri ATCC 33323, which produces GLP-1 protein, their blood glucose levels decreased by 33%. Similarly, altered L. lactis FI5876 was reassembled to biosynthesize and distribute incretin hormone GLP-1, which stimulates β-cell insulin secretion under high glucose levels.

4.3 Synthetic biology in artificial organelles:-

Synthetic biology principles can be applied to self-assemble organelles, mimicking characteristics of living cells like enzyme reaction compartmentalization and stimuli-responses. Combining artificial organelles with engineered living cell chassis can enhance therapeutic results or control artificial systems. Polymersomes, hollow vesicles made from amphiphilic polymers, can be used as shells for artificial organelles. These organelles can protect cells from reactive oxidative molecules and protect against H2O2 damage radicals. The study confirmed the feasibility of creating an artificial organelle with catalase activity. Engineered polymersomes could potentially treat medical diseases. Artificial organelles can treat several diseases, such as Parkinson's, Alzheimer's, Huntington's, metabolic disorders, malignancies, and acatalasemia, by storing therapeutic proteins.

Combining nanobiotechnology and synthetic biology can enable new functions. Researchers can build "artificial lives" by assembling nanoparticles according to the "bottle" method.
The "up" principle. The concept can be used to create biological components with inorganic scaffolding and functional nanomaterials that include nucleic acids and proteins.The "top-down" method can guide the usage of nanomaterials in living cells to enhance robustness, stability, and sensitivity for medical applications.

4.4 In drug delivery

Advances in nanotechnology offer more targeted and controllable-release DNA/RNA delivery systems, addressing safety concerns and enhancing therapeutic agents and genome engineering tools. Liposome nanomaterials have become an effective gene therapy method, with various artificial lipid vectors approved for clinical use. Liposomes are small lipid vesicles used for delivering drugs, reducing drug toxicity and delivering drugs directly to targets. They are also used in CRISPR/Cas9-aided gene therapies, integrating negatively charged mRNA, gRNA scaffolds, and CRISPR genes with positively charged liposomes via electrostatic interactions. Liposomes have also been used to deliver mRNA encoding SARS-CoV-2 antigens to humans as vaccines.

4.5 Biological Computers:-

Biological computers are designed biological systems that can execute computer-like processes, marking a significant shift in synthetic biology research. Scientists have successfully developed and examined logic gates in diverse creatures, demonstrating analog and digital processing capabilities in live cells. Researchers have demonstrated that bacteria can be engineered to perform both analog and digital computations, paving the way for advanced biological computing.

4.6 Biosensor:-

Biosensors are used to detect pathogens in food. The presence of Escherichia coli in vegetables indicates faecal contamination in meals. E. coli was detected utilizing potentiometric alternating biosensing systems, which detect variations in pH caused by ammonia (generated by urease-E. coli antibody conjugates). We obtain the liquid phase by washing vegetables such as sliced carrots and lettuce with peptone water. It is then separated by blending it in a sonicator to remove bacterial cells from food.Enzymatic biosensors are also used in the dairy business. A flow cell was outfitted with a biosensor built around a screen-printed carbon electrode. Enzymes were fixed on electrodes by engulfing them in a photocrosslinking polymer. The automated flow-based biosensor could quantify the three organophosphates pesticides in milk..

References :-

1.Garner KL. Principles of synthetic biology. *Essays Biochem.* 2021;65(5):791-811. doi:10.1042/EBC20200059

2.Acevedo-Rocha CG. The synthetic nature of biology. In: *Ambivalences of Creating Life: Societal and Philosophical Dimensions of Synthetic Biology.* Springer International Publishing; 2015:9-53. doi:10.1007/ 978-3-319-21088-9_2

3. deplazes-2009-piecing-together-a-puzzle.

4. Paddon CJ, Westfall PJ, Pitera DJ, et al. High-level semi-synthetic production of the potent antimalarial artemisinin. *Nature.*

2013;496(7446):528-532. doi:10.1038/nature12051

CHAPTER SEVEN

DECODING LIFE: EXPLORING BIOINFORMATICS

In the realm of healthcare, advancements in technology have catalysed a transformative shift towards personalized medicine. The multidisciplinary field of bioinformatics, which skilfully combines biology, computer science, and information technology to decode complicated biological data, is at the front of this change. With its unparalleled ability to provide insights into a person's genetic composition, underlying disease processes, and response to treatment, bioinformatics has become a key component in the push for personalised medicine. Here we will see how bioinformatics is transforming healthcare paradigms, advancing the discovery and application of personalised medications, and enhancing patient outcomes.

1. Introduction:-

The use of living things or biological molecules to develop new technologies or produce new, commercially appealing products is known as biotechnology, and it has spread to a variety of industries, including medicine, health, plant and animal breeding, the production of biofuel, and many more. Advances in these fields, which have resulted in the creation of "omics" technologies, have been made possible by the immense potential presented by the development of molecular biology, genetic engineering tools, computational advancements, and new technologies for DNA sequencing and liquid/mass spectroscopy. Knowledge of genomics and transcriptomics has grown exponentially as a result of the rapid development of data analysis techniques spurred by advances in molecular biology, particularly through DNA sequencing technology. Highly analytical and comprehensive methodologies like high-resolution, time-resolved bioimaging analysis and omics analysis have emerged as a result of recent advancements. A single measurement can now yield a large amount of data thanks to these technologies.

Together with significant advancements in the use of crystallography to determine protein structures, the first protein sequence—that is, the arrangement of amino acids in a chain—was published for the protein insulin in the late 1950s. This significant development ended the discussion regarding the order of proteins' polypeptide chains.It also promoted the creation of more effective techniques for collecting protein sequences. One amino acid at a time, beginning at the N-terminus, protein sequencing was made possible with the advent of the straightforward Edman degradation process. Over the next ten years, more than fifteen distinct protein families were sequenced in conjunction with automation .Obtaining big protein sequences posed a significant challenge for Edman sequencing. Using phenylisothiocyanate, Edman sequencing cleaves N-terminal amino acid residues one at a time. Nevertheless, this reaction's yield is never fully achieved. This makes it possible to sequence up to 50–60 amino acids in a single Edman reaction. It is necessary to break larger proteins into smaller pieces, which are subsequently isolated and sequenced separately.

American physical chemist Margaret Dayhoff (1925–1983) was a trailblazer in the field of biochemistry when it came to using computational approaches. David J. Lipman, a former director of the National Center for Biotechnology Information (NCBI), referred to Dayhoff as "the mother and father of bioinformatics" because of the significance of her contributions to this discipline. Together, they put their skills to use between 1958 and 1962 to create COMPROTEIN, "a complete computer program for the IBM 7090" that used Edman peptide sequencing data to determine the main structure of proteins .This program, which was created entirely on punch cards using FORTRAN, is the original example of a de novo sequence assembler.

Although the mechanistic modeling of enzymes was the main emphasis of biochemistry research up to the 1960s, Emile Zuckerkandl and Linus Pauling broke with this paradigm by examining biomolecular sequences as "carriers of information." Similar to how words are composed of letters whose precise order conveys meaning, a protein's molecular function—that is, its meaning—is determined by the arrangement of its amino acids to form a "word." The first dynamic programming approach for pairwise protein sequence alignments was created in 1970 by Needleman and Wunsch. Da-Fei Feng and Russell F. Doolitle developed the first practical MSA approach in 1987, 'progressive sequence alignment', which involved Needleman-Wunsch alignment, extracting similarity scores, building a guide tree, and aligning sequences.

The double helix was discovered in 1953, the first DNA sequencing was carried out in 1968 (Hutchison 2007). On the other hand, Sanger's dideoxy approach and Maxam and Gilbert's chemical method started in the middle of the 1970s. With the first complete DNA sequence of phage ϕX174, Nicklen and Coulson demonstrated important insights into genetic organization. Larger molecules, like the human cytomegalovirus, which weighed more than 200 kb, could be sequenced as sequencing output increased, giving rise to computational analysis and bioinformatics. The polymerase chain reaction (PCR), which enables DNA amplification without the need for cloning processes, was the second major advancement in DNA manipulation. While Kjell Kleppe et al. initially described the use of DNA polymerase for "repair synthesis" in 1971.

The advancement of Sanger sequencing and the development of additional high-throughput sequencing techniques led to a significant increase in our understanding of genomes.With the completion of the Human Genome Project's (HGP) sequencing of the entire human genome in 2003, there is now hope for the diagnosis and treatment of genetic illnesses affecting people. The research was successful, finishing three years ahead of schedule and ten percent under budget with 1631 known DNA sequences. The project's success was facilitated by innovations in molecular biology, engineering, robotics, statistical techniques, and computer systems, which also acted as a breeding ground for multidisciplinary research. The development of DNA-microarray technology has opened up new avenues for the investigation of molecular pathways associated with human illness. However, as basic sciences have advanced through the application of genomic techniques, so too have analytical and bioinformatics issues arisen.

Acknowledging the intrinsic diversity among people with respect to genetic susceptibilities and environmental factors is fundamental to the personalised medicine idea. Conventional medical practices sometimes take a "one-size-fitsall" stance, prescribing uniform therapies based on averages for large populations. This method, however, ignores the distinct genetic profiles and physiological variations that affect therapy efficiency and illness vulnerability. This gap is filled by bioinformatics, which uses state-of-the-art computer tools and algorithms to analyse enormous volumes of biological data, including molecular pathways and genomic sequences. Genomic analysis is one of the main uses of bioinformatics in personalised medicine. Billions of nucleotides make up the human genome, and each one contains important genetic information. With the aid of bioinformatics pipelines and high-throughput sequencing technology, scientists can decode this genetic code with previously unheard-of precision and speed. Through the identification of genetic variations linked to medication metabolism or illness susceptibility, medical professionals can customise treatment plans to meet the individual needs of each patient. Pharmacogenomics, for example, uses genetic information to forecast a person's reaction to different treatments, allowing doctors to recommend the safest and most efficient ones for a given patient.

Moreover, bioinformatics is essential for understanding the molecular processes that underlie complicated disorders. Researchers can obtain a thorough understanding of disease pathophysiology at the molecular level by combining genomic data with other omics disciplines including transcriptomics, proteomics, and metabolomics. This integrated method reveals putative therapeutic targets for drug development in addition to clarifying the complex interactions between genes, proteins, and metabolic pathways. For example, by identifying the driving mutations and signalling pathways that cause carcinogenesis, cancer genomics has transformed oncology and made targeted medicines and precision oncology methodologies possible. Bioinformatics advances preventative medicine by enabling early detection of illness risk factors and facilitating personalised interventions, in addition to diagnosis and therapy. Researchers are able to examine large datasets and find patterns and trends that may indicate a propensity to disease by using predictive modelling and machine learning techniques. Predictive analytics can create personalised risk profiles by combining genetic, environmental, and lifestyle factors. This allows people to take proactive steps to reduce their chance of contracting specific diseases. Furthermore, precision screening tactics that give priority to patients at higher risk are made possible by bioinformatics-driven methodologies, which optimise resource allocation and healthcare delivery. A number of obstacles must be overcome before personalised medicine may be implemented, such as legislative barriers, privacy concerns, and data integration issues. Significant computational and analytical hurdles are brought about by the sheer volume and complexity of biological data produced by omics technologies and genome sequencing. The ever-increasing volume of data requires bioinformatics tools and algorithms to adapt quickly in order to guarantee precise interpretation and useful insights. Furthermore, in the age of big data and linked healthcare systems, protecting the confidentiality and security of personal health information is critical. Maintaining data integrity and protecting individual rights demands strong governance structures and ethical principles that strike a balance between patient confidentiality and data accessibility.

Moreover, regulatory approval and validation through rigorous clinical studies are necessary for the translation of discoveries led by bioinformatics into clinical practice. To protect patient safety and public confidence, regulatory bodies like the FDA are essential in assessing the efficacy, safety, and quality of personalised medicine therapies. Personalised medicine has a bright future ahead of it, thanks to developments in precision healthcare technologies and bioinformatics. A paradigm change towards more accurate, efficient, and patient-centred healthcare is provided by personalised medicine, which uses bioinformatics to decipher the intricacies of the human genome and molecular pathways. Bioinformatics will stay at the vanguard of innovation as we continue to solve the riddles surrounding human biology and disease. It will power the next wave of personalised medications that improve lives and push the envelope on what constitutes excellent healthcare.

Other sciences that have an integrated molecular biology interface, such bioinformatics and computational biology, are born or evolve alongside the "new biology" era. Bioinformatics and genomics have developed in tandem and had a historical influence on the body of knowledge, despite their recent consideration. As a result, the purpose of this chapter is to give a succinct synopsis of these fields and to offer guiding principles for bioinformatics that cover the following areas: Molecular Biology,Types biological data and databases, molecular modeling and sequence analysis, genomic analysis.

2. Molecular biology:-

The study of biology at the molecular level is called molecular biology. The fields of biology, chemistry, and especially genetics and biochemistry share some overlap. Understanding the relationships between a cell's many processes, such as those involving DNA (deoxyribonucleic acid), RNA (ribonucleic acid), and protein production, as well as how these interactions are regulated, is the main focus of molecular biology.

Nowadays, the majority of genetic material in living things is DNA. The most important study on DNA structure was published by Watson and Crick a little more than 60 years ago. They highlighted two key characteristics of the molecule in it: the polymer's double helix structure and the complementarity of the base sequences on the two strands. Base sequence complementarity—adenine complementary to thymine and guanine complementary to cytosine—offered a sophisticated molecular explanation for the finding made by Avery, McCarty, and Macleod a decade earlier that DNA was most likely the "transforming principle" that allowed genetic information to be transferred between various strains of Abbreviations bacteria. Furthermore, it supported Chargaff's basic discovery that the nucleotides A and T and G and C in double-stranded DNA are equivalent (Figure 1).

Thus, compared to the minor groove, the major groove offers more sequence information. A-DNA and B-DNA (Fig. 2) are the two types of right-handed double-helical structures that DNA can adopt, whereas RNA can only assemble into an A-type double helix due to the steric constraints placed on ribose by the 20 hydroxyl residue. The Watson and Crick-proposed B-DNA structure is most stable at high humidities, but when the water activity is reduced, it changes into the A-form. According to this theory, direct access to DNA sequence information is made possible by the capacity to adopt the B-form . DNA coding capacity can be achieved through various base pairs, such as A-T and G-C, DAP-T(diaminopurine–thymine) and H-C (hypoxanthine–cytosine), or all-two or three hydrogen bonds. These variations affect protein recognition and thermal stability, as well as the molecule's physicochemical properties.

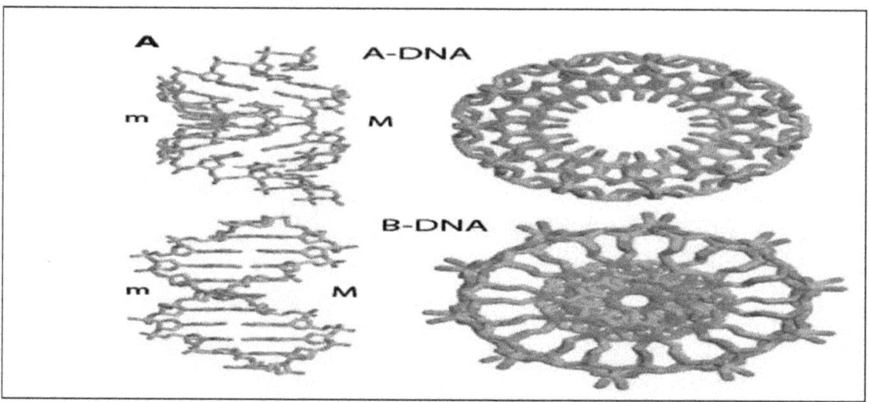

According to the RNA World Hypothesis, RNA rather than DNA and proteins was the primary component of primordial life. RNA has remained essential to cell life over the course of 4 billion years, despite the fact that modern cells have undergone tremendous modification. RNA has been thoroughly investigated since the end of the nineteenth century, when DNA was discovered. The messenger RNA model, which was developed in the late 1950s and is the cornerstone of the basic dogma of molecular biology, was backed by several discoveries, including housekeeping RNAs (rRNA, tRNA, etc.). The first regulatory non-coding RNAs (ncRNAs) were discovered thirty years later, first in bacteria and subsequently in the majority of eukaryotic creatures.

All ribonucleic acids are transcripts at the start of their cellular lives. An transcript should be considered an RNA if it, or any byproduct of its processing, serves a purpose. Transcripts (class 0) could be used to refer to nonfunctional transcripts, by-products of processing, degradation intermediates, even those derived from (functional) RNAs, and non-functional products of transcriptional gene regulation achieved through the act of transcription. Numerous functional RNAs (class I) are organized into ever-expanding subclassifications, ranging from micro RNAs to rRNAs. These subclassifications often mature after one or more processing steps. Well-established subclassifications that cover a broad range of functional variety are unaltered. Because mRNAs (class II) have the ability to be translated into (poly)peptide(s) on ribosomes, they stand apart from all other RNA.

One of the most significant classes of molecules for life, proteins form the basis of the study of biochemistry. One of the four main molecules that govern life is a protein. The other three are lipids (fats), polysaccharides (sugars), and nucleic acids (deoxyribonucleic acid, or DNA).These massive "macromolecules" are all carbon-based covalent compounds that engage and fold with their targets through weak reversible non-covalent interactions, giving the individual molecules and their complexes unique forms and dynamics. While shorter polypeptides (less than 30 amino acids) are usually referred to as peptides, proteins are polymers of often hundreds of amino acids bound together by peptide bonds. Every amino acid shares an identical structure with a core α carbon atom. ($C\alpha$) conjugated to amino groups ($-NH2$) and carboxylic acid groups ($-COOH$), both of which are utilized in the formation of peptide bonds.The most intriguing part is that the $C\alpha$ group is attached to a distinct R group for 19 out of the 20 amino acids, meaning that each amino acid has its own distinct "side chain." Because side chains vary in size, shape, polarity, charge, and hydrophobicity, they provide amino acids their unique structural and chemical characteristics. The sidechains and backbone groups of a polypeptide chain interact with one another through a variety of weak interactions, such as hydrogen bonds, van der Waals, electrostatic interactions, and the hydrophobic effect, to determine the shape and target interactions of the protein.

3. Computational Tools:-

Currently, there are a variety of bioinformatics tools accessible, each tailored to meet a particular purpose in biological research. The structure and level of sophistication of bioinformatics tools varies, from straightforward command-line tools to intricate graphical applications and stand-alone online services. Annotations, pathways, illness information, genetic and protein sequences, and other biological data are all archived in biological databases. These databases are used to store and arrange information so that it may be easily retrieved. Primary databases are sets of raw sequences or structural data that have not been processed in any way. These databases contain only authentic information and aren't altered in any way. Secondary database Data that has been manually or computationally processed and vetted is found in secondary databases. These databases' contents are derived from primary databases' original data.

3.1 Entrez:-

The system is an integrated database search and retrieval system that uses Boolean expressions for text searching. It integrates data from various sources, creating a uniform information model for indexing and retrieval. It provides access to sequential, structural, and taxonomic data, chromosome maps, and related sequences, structures, or references.

3.2 PubMed:-

The PubMed database, which is a component of the NCBI Entrez retrieval system, was created by the NCBI National Library of Medicine (NLM) to make it simpler for users to retrieve abstracts and references from publications in the biomedical and life sciences.

3.3 Protein:-

Individual protein sequences are stored in this database in textual formats such as XML and FASTA. The NCBI Reference Sequence (RefSeq) project, GenBank, and PDB and SWISS-Prot are the most popular sites from which these sequences have been obtained.

3.4 GenBank:-

Since 1992, the USA-based NCBI has made the GenBank DNA sequence database freely accessible. NCBI works with GenBank, EMBL, and DDBJ to update their databases with the most recent discoveries.

3.5 KEGG:-

(Kyoto Encyclopedia of Genes and Genomes) is a biological database that provides molecular-level knowledge regarding a variety of cellular processes, including as metabolism, signaling, and illnesses. It also includes genomic, chemical, and systemic functional information.

3.6 OMIM:-

With approximately 16,000 genes and comprehensive, referenced summaries of all known Mendelian genetic disorders, Online Mendelian Inheritance in Man (OMIM) is a publicly accessible library of human genes and genetic disorders.

3.7 Gene Expression Omnibus (GEO):-

It can be characterized as a system for storing and retrieving different kinds of high-throughput molecular abundance data. It accepts data from gene expression, SNP arrays, chromatin immune precipitation on arrays (ChIP-chips), and array comparative genomic hybridization (aCGH).

3.8 Online Mendelian Inheritance in Animals (OMIA):-

It is a database that includes features, genetic illnesses, and characteristics of animals other than humans and mice. Additionally, it contains connections to pertinent entries in the PubMed, OMIM, and Gene databases.

3.9 PubChem:-

Using Microsoft SQL servers to generate its relational databases, PubChem can be thought of as a molecular library. In order for small molecules to be employed as therapeutic and diagnostic agents, their biological, chemical, and structural characteristics are the main areas of study. Access to all of the deposited data is available freely by the users. It is composed of three sub-databases: PCSubstance, PCCompound, and PCBioAssay. These sub-databases contain information about substances, compound structures, and compound bioactivity, respectively.

4. Gene prediction tool:-

4.1 GeneMark:-

Using a non-homogeneous Markov model to categorize DNA sections into protein-coding, non-coding, and non-coding but complementary to coding categories, GeneMark was the first tool for identifying prokaryotic genes. Previous research has demonstrated that the E. coli genes may be categorized into three gene sets using multivariate codon use analysis: typical, highly typical, and atypical. The latter two groups appear to correspond to highly expressed genes and horizontally transmitted genes.

4.2 Glimmer:-

Steven Salzberg and others at Johns Hopkins University and TIGR created the Gene Locator and Interpolated Markov Modeler, a tool for locating genes in bacterial genomes. Glimmer employs interpolated Markov models—a sequence of Markov models with the order of the model rising at each step and the prediction value of each model independently evaluated—to find coding regions and segregate them from noncoding DNA.

4.3 Grail:-

Identification and Assembly of Genes By comparing DNA sequences to a database of known human and mouse sequence elements, Internet Link, a tool created by Ed Uberbacher and colleagues at the Oak Ridge National Laboratory, can identify exons, polyA sites, promoters, CpG islands, repetitive elements, and frameshift errors.

4.4 GeneScan:-

Chris Burge and Samuel Karlin of Stanford University created GenScan. This software makes use of an intricate probabilistic model of the gene structure, grounded in real biological data regarding the characteristics of translational, splicing, and transcriptional signals. It also makes use of different statistical characteristics of coding and noncoding areas. GenScan generates several sets of gene models for genome areas with varying GC content in order to take into consideration the variability of the human genome, which influences gene density and gene organization . GenScan is the preferred technique for the preliminary examination of extensive (within the megabase range) segments of eukaryotic genomic DNA due to its exceptional speed and precision. The International Human Genome Project has employed GenScan as its primary tool for gene prediction.

4.5 GeneBuilder:-

GeneBuilder uses a variety of criteria, including GC content, dicodon frequencies, splicing site information, CpG islands, repetitive regions, and more, to do ab initio gene prediction. In order to determine plausible coding sequences, it also employs a novel technique based on comparing the relative frequency of synonymous and nonsynonymous changes. Furthermore, it runs BLAST searches of anticipated genes against EST and protein databases, which aids in fine-tuning the projected exon boundaries by using the BLAST results as a reference. By allowing the user to modify specific parameters, the application facilitates interactive gene structure prediction. Because of this, GeneBuilder can occasionally accurately predict the gene structure even in cases when the predicted ORF has little match to a homologous protein sequence.

4.6 Sequence Analysis Tools:-

These instruments are employed for the analysis of protein or nucleotide sequences. They are also employed in the identification of homologous sequences and the comprehension of the evolutionary connections among various creatures. These comprise tools for phylogeny, motif identification, genome assembly and comparison, sequence alignment, and sequence database searches. Several widely used tools for sequence analysis include

4.7 ClustalW:-

A multiple sequence alignment tool for DNA and protein sequences is called ClustalW.

4.8 T-Coffee:-

Another popular multiple sequence alignment tool is T-Coffee, which generates precise alignments by combining progressive and consistency-based alignment techniques. It works very well for aligning sequences that are far apart.

4.9 MEME:-

For motif search and discovery, MEME (Multiple EM for Motif Elicitation) is utilized. The four types of motif analysis that the MEME Suite software tools does are motif discovery, motif-sequence database searching, motif–motif database searching, and assignment of function.

4.10 MEGA:-

Multiple sequence alignment, model selection, and tree inference are just a few of the many phylogenetic analysis techniques available in the user-friendly program MEGA (Molecular Evolutionary Genetics Analysis).

4.11 PHYLIP:-

A group of computer programs called PHYLIP (Phylogeny Inference Package) are used to ascertain the evolutionary relationships between species.

5. Structure Analysis Tools:-

5.1 CN3D :-

A software program called CN3D is used to see and examine the three-dimensional structures of macromolecules, such as proteins and nucleic acids. It offers resources for displaying and interacting with macromolecules' three-dimensional structure.

5.2 PyMOL:-

PyMOL is a molecular visualization program used for animation, analysis, and visualization of three-dimensional molecular structures. It can show molecules as surface representations, cartoons, or ball-and-stick models, among other formats.,

5.3 RasMol :-

Designed to view and show proteins, nucleic acids, and tiny molecules in a graphical style is a molecular graphics tool.

5.4 ODELLER :-

Protein structures can be predicted using ODELLER, a comparative protein structure modeling tool, by comparing the new structure to an existing protein structure.

6. CORE LABORATORY TECHNOLOGIES

New technical developments that make it possible to quickly and affordably collect different kinds of data are a major driving force behind genome science. The field has been described as being more data-driven than hypothesis-driven, which is a reflection of researchers' propensity to gather vast amounts of genomic data in the (realistic) hope that further data analysis and the experiments they recommend will improve our understanding of genetic processes.

6.1 Gene Sequencing:-

DNA sequences have an orientation. The 5' end of a sequence might be considered the left end, while the 3' end is on the right. Sanger sequencing begins by generating all feasible subsequences of the target sequence that start with the same 5' nucleotide. A reporter, which was originally radioactive but is now fluorescent, is linked to each subsequence's last 3' nucleotide. The final 3' nucleotide in each subsequence can be identified by utilizing a unique reporter for each of the four nucleotides. Consider sequencing the DNA molecule AGGT. There are four potential subsequences starting with the 5' A: A, AG, AGG, and AGGT.

Sanger sequencing generates each of these four sequences and binds the reporter to the last nucleotide. The subsequences are ordered from shortest to longest depending on their migration rate via a medium. The shortest sequence corresponds to the subsequence A; the reporter indicates that the final nucleotide is an A. The second shortest subsequence is AG, which ends with a G. By arranging the subsequences in a "ladder" from shortest to longest, the sequence of the whole target sequence can be obtained simply by reading off the final nucleotide of each subsequence.

Advances in Sanger sequencing have permitted high-throughput sequencing of whole genomes, including human genomes. Radioactive reporters have been replaced by safer fluorescent dyes, and automated laser-based systems read sequences directly. Modern sequencing machines can scan sequences of at least 800 nucleotides. Capillary sequencers and robotic equipment have enabled nearly fully automated sequencing pathways. Automated base-calling algorithms, such as phred, can produce highly accurate DNA sequences while reducing human interaction. A single DNA sequencing machine can generate up to a million nucleotides every day.

6.2 Gene Expression:-

Following high-throughput genome sequencing, scientists were able to assess the relative abundance of thousands of different gene products. These technologies are essentially a high-throughput substitute for the Northern blot method. The assays provide a quantitative estimate of the quantity of mRNA copies produced in a specific tissue for each member of a collection of several thousand genes. Currently, two technologies dominate the field: cDNA and oligonucleotide microarrays, which have enabled many previously unthinkable exploratory investigations.

cDNA microarrays are high-throughput gene expression methods that attach DNA sequences of thousands of genes onto microscope slides in a pattern of spots. Various technologies have been developed for creating these slides. The RNA of expressed genes is collected from the target cell population, and a cDNA version of each RNA is created through reverse transcription. The cDNA collection is labeled with fluorescent dye, and the number of bound molecules at each spot is measured.

Oligonucleotide arrays use short oligonucleotides specific to individual genes, with approximately 10-20 different oligonucleotides printed onto a chip for each gene. This reduces potential errors and allows fluorescently labeled RNA to be hybridized against the array. However, only a single sample can be assayed on a single chip.

6.3 Sequence analysis:-

Paul Berg, Frederick Sanger, and Walter Gilbert's pioneering work on DNA sequencing resulted in the creation of Sanger sequencing, a technology that revolutionized DNA research. Over the last two decades, major breakthroughs, particularly in nanotechnology and informatics, have contributed to a new generation of sequencing technologies. These novel approaches aimed to supplement and eventually replace Sanger sequencing. This technology is known as next-generation sequencing (NGS) or massively parallel sequencing (MPS), which is frequently used as an umbrella term to describe a wide range of methodologies. This technique allows you to generate huge amounts of data per instrument run in a faster and more cost-effective method, streaming the parallel study of many genes or even the entire genome.

In addition to sequencing DNA, another interesting application of capillary electrophoresis on the AB machines has been the invention of methods for assaying the activity of selected enzymes functioning on fluorescently tagged DNA substrates, by analyzing, for example, DNA fragment size. The term "next generation" refers to the next stage in DNA sequencing technology, while new technologies are commonly referred to as second or third generation. Automated AB sequencing machine technology is classified as the second generation, following the original Sanger methods. Second-generation technologies, such Solid and Polinator, provide higher throughput sequencing at a cheaper cost. Second-generation sequencing technologies are divided into two categories: hybridization and sequencing by synthesis (SBS). SBS methods are a further evolution of Sanger sequencing, omitting the dideoxy terminators and combining repeated cycles of synthesis, imaging, and ways for incorporating more nucleotides into the expanding chain.

6.4 Sequencing via hybridization :-

This method was first developed in the 1980s, with arrayed DNA oligonucleotides of known sequence on filters that were hybridized to tagged pieces of the DNA to be sequenced. By repeatedly hybridizing and washing away non-hybridized DNA, it was possible to assess if the hybridizing tagged fragments matched the sequence of the DNA probes on the filter. It was thus able to construct bigger continuous sequence information using overlapping information from the probe hybridization sites. Sequencing by hybridization has been largely relegated to technologies that rely on the use of specific probes to interrogate sequences, such as in diagnostic applications for identifying disease-related SNPS (single-nucleotide polymorphisms) in specific genes or identifying gross chromosome abnormalities.

6.5 Sequencing by Synthesis (SBS):-

Current Sanger sequencing (SBS) technologies have a greater error rate and rely on short DNA sequence reads, which might number in the millions or billions. However, some technologies encounter sequence context issues, such as homopolymer sequences, which cannot always be rectified by increasing the number of reads. To solve these difficulties, SBS technologies are currently concentrating on developing technologies that create longer primary read lengths while retaining the technology's "massively parallel" nature. Most SBS technologies employ a procedure in which individual DNA molecules are distributed to millions of independent wells or chambers and amplified using PCR or isothermal modified amplification techniques. Several innovative technologies have been developed to generate millions of DNA sequence reads in a single sequence run.

Most SBS technologies use a procedure in which individual DNA molecules to be sequenced are distributed to millions of different wells or chambers, or anchored to specific spots on a solid substrate. After being amplified by PCR or isothermal modified "rolling circle" amplification methods, the DNA molecules are subjected to DNA synthesis reactions that allow tagged nucleotides, or chemical reactions depending on the incorporation of a specific nucleotide, to be imaged or detected. Several innovative technologies have been developed to generate millions of DNA sequence reads in a single sequence run. Depending on the throughput, sequence runs might last from hours to several days.

6.6 Ion Torrent:-

The Ion Torrent™ technology transforms nucleotide sequences into digital information on a semiconductor chip. In DNA synthesis, incorporating the right nucleotide changes the pH of the solution, which can be measured as a voltage change by an ion sensor. Sequencing regents flood and wash the chamber, causing voltage fluctuations and determining "runs" of a single nucleotide.

6.7 Illumina technology:-

Illumina is the market leader in second-generation sequencing employing "bridge amplification" technology. This includes placing DNA molecules with adapters on a glass slide containing oligonucleotide sequences. This generates clonal clusters containing 1000 copies of each oligonucleotide fragment. During synthesis, modified nucleotides bearing various fluorescent labels are inserted and detected. The reactions are repeated 300 or more times, with fluorescence detection increasing detection speed.

6.8 PacBio SMRT:-

Pacific Biosciences (PacBio) is a technical leader in third-generation sequencing methods, particularly SMRT (Single Molecule Real Time) sequencing. This approach enables the sequencing of lengthy DNA and RNA molecules of up to 30-50 kb. The procedure entails connecting a designed DNA polymerase to the bottom of a well (zero-mode waveguide) in an SMRT flow cell, where it integrates each base in a developing chain.

The four nucleotides are labeled with separate phospho-linked fluorophores to aid in detection. Imaging takes place on a millisecond time scale as the proper fluorescently labeled nucleotide is attached. The method also includes the creation of a "SMRTbell," a circular double-stranded DNA molecule with a known adaptor sequence that complements the primers used to start DNA synthesis on the template. This This allows the polymerase to read through big templates multiple times, traversing the circular molecule in each ZMW until it stops, resulting in a consensus sequence (CCS). PacBio SMRT sequencing has various advantages over earlier technologies, including the ability to quickly identify methylation sites for epigenetic investigations and provide long reads for genome assemblies. The latest PacBio device, the Sequel, contains 1 million ZMWs and can output approximately 365,000 readings.

7. Application:-

7.1 Detection of Tumor Viruses:-

Computational subtraction analysis was utilized to detect viral sequences in EST libraries and post-transplant lymphoproliferative disease tissue. This approach was used to identify a novel polyomavirus linked to Merkel cell carcinoma (MCC), a rare and severe human skin disease. The identification of a fusion transcript between a human receptor tyrosine phosphatase and a Large T antigen sequence linked to mouse polyomaviruses resulted in the characterisation of Merkel cell polyomavirus. The virus's presence in 80% of MCC tissues, as well as its clonal integration into the tumor genome, suggest a role in MCC pathogenesis. A NGS investigation discovered a human polyomavirus strain in an MCC patient that was comparable to HPyV9 and closely related to LSV. High-throughput sequencing and deep amplicon sequencing resulted in the identification of novel polyomavirus and papillomavirus genotypes.

The Papillomaviridae family contains 189 known papillomavirus types, and new ones are constantly discovered. High-throughput 454 pyrosequencing was utilized to detect and genotype HPV in cervical cytology specimens as well as cutaneous HPV types in squamous cell carcinoma, resulting in the identification of numerous new types, including novel putative HPVs. The study of retrovirus and retroviral vector integration sites in host cell chromosomes is an area of viral oncology that has substantially benefited from NGS technologies. These locations can promote malignant transformation when viral vectors integrate into host genes. Deep sequencing techniques, such as 454 pyrosequencing, have been utilized to pinpoint these locations for gene therapy and cell reprogramming. A new approach, based on the bacterial transposase MuA, has been devised to retrieve sites of integrated DNA while eliminating bias caused by restriction enzymes and providing a measure of cell clonal abundance.

7.2 Identification of Allergens in Food:-

Bioinformatics can help to identify allergens in food, improving food safety for allergy sufferers. By analyzing common allergen genomes, producers can develop products less likely to cause reactions and improve labeling.

7.3 Monitoring Antiviral Drug Resistance:-

Deep sequencing with NGS techniques is rapidly being employed in clinical practice to detect low-abundance drug-resistant HIV variants and HCV minor mutations. Conventional direct sequencing, the gold standard in HIV resistance testing, can only reveal drug-resistant variations in less than 20-25% of the viral population. Minor variations not discovered by population-based sequencing are clinically significant and can lead to therapy failure. 454 pyrosequencing is a technology for clonal sequencing of RT-PCR results that provides great sensitivity for small changes and a lengthy sequence length for characterizing resistance mutations. However, it necessitates a detailed examination of technical mistakes in experimental techniques and data analysis. Studies have demonstrated its ability to detect drug-resistance mutations in HIV protease and reverse transcriptase genes, with some having a major impact on virological failure.

Deep sequencing can discover drug-resistant mutations in the integrase gene at low levels prior to therapy. HIV mutations that target CXCR4 cause resistance to CCR5 antagonists. Phenotypic and genotypic tests are useful but time-consuming and costly. Population sequencing is a viable option, but it has lesser sensitivity for minority mutations. Deep sequencing with 454 has been utilized in research to detect viral tropism and offers similar sensitivity and specificity to phenotypic testing. With a clinical threshold of 2-10%, 454 pyrosequencing can be a useful diagnostic technique for viral tropism analysis. Deep sequencing with 454 technology was used to detect nucleoside and nucleotide reverse transcriptase inhibitor resistance in HBV, detecting uncommon mutations more sensitively than traditional approaches. Deep sequencing also revealed G-to-A hypermutation in 0.6% of reverse transcriptase genes. With new medications targeting HCV protease and polymerase, deep sequencing methods provide fresh insights into HCV resistance dynamics.

7.4 Identifying new drug targets:-

Bioinformatics is critical in drug discovery and development because it allows for the identification of new drug targets through the analysis of huge biological datasets. This includes assessing gene expression data from cancer patients, identifying proteins involved in disease processes, and employing high-throughput screening tests to test compounds against targets, resulting in the identification of effective treatments.

References:-

1. Muse S. GENOMICS AND BIOINFORMATICS. In: *Introduction to Biomedical Engineering.* Elsevier; 2005:799-831. doi:10.1016/B978-0-12-238662-6.50015-X

2. Travers A, Muskhelishvili G. DNA structure and function. *FEBS Journal.* 2015;282(12):2279-2295. doi:10.1111/febs.13307

NATURE'S ENGINEERS: HARNESSING ENVIRONMENTAL BIOTECHNOLOGY FOR A SUSTAINABLE FUTURE

Introduction

In an era where environmental challenges loom large, the field of biotechnology emerges as a beacon of hope. Nature, with its intricate web of organisms and processes, has long been the ultimate engineer, adept at finding ingenious solutions to complex problems. Environmental biotechnology leverages the power of living organisms and bioprocesses to tackle pollution, mitigate climate change, and promote sustainability. This chapter explores the remarkable potential of environmental biotechnology to shape a greener, more sustainable future.

The term "environmental biotechnology" encapsulates a wide and dynamic spectrum of topics including bioremediation, biofiltration, wastewater treatment, biodegradation, waste management, and biofuel production. All these disciplines are underpinned by complex interacting microbial communities; hence exciting research has been undertaken and increasingly driven by cutting-edge ecogenomic techniques. However, understanding of microbial diversity, population, and structure for sustainable environmental management remains largely a "black box." Thus exciting findings identified new knowledge gaps and, inevitably, engendered novel research questions with inventive methodologies.

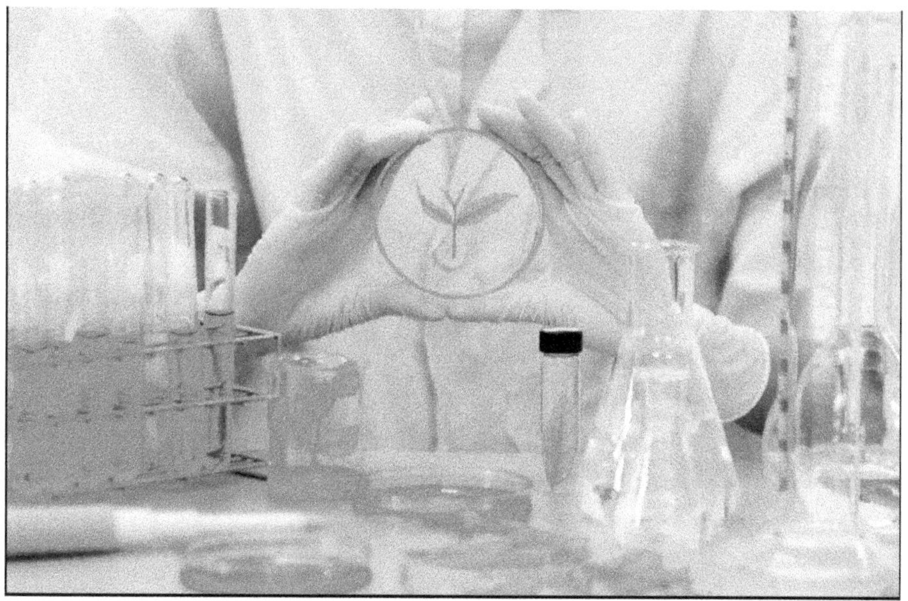

In recent years, the demand for the use of sustainable and eco-friendly environmental processes is rapidly growing subjected to economic, public, and legislation pressure. Biotechnology provides a plethora of opportunities for effectively addressing issues pertaining to the monitoring, assessment, modeling, and treatment of contaminated water, air, and solid waste streams. In this context, source tracking of environmental pollutants and process modeling using biological based methods are becoming increasingly important, mainly owing to the accuracy and robustness of such techniques. The different biotechniques available nowadays, thus, represent both well-established and novel (bio)technologies, although several aspects of their performance are still to be tested. For instance, the use of novel biocatalysts and reactor designs, the understanding of microbial community dynamics and mechanisms occurring within a (bio)reactor, and the assessment of the performance of (bio)reactors during long-term operation and its modeling. If these mechanisms are understood and the barriers are overcome, novel biotechniques will potentially change the way users rebuild technologies for the sustainable use of different biological processes for wastewater, air, and solid waste treatment.

Environmental Monitoring and Modeling. In developing countries, water, air, and soil pollution has become a persisting environmental problem due to rapid industrialization and urbanization. Using environmental Kuznets curve (EKC) it was observed that, during early stages of economic development in a particular region, the environment paid a high price for economic growth as the human race used technology to exploit all possible valuable resources. Nevertheless, in agricultural areas, N, P, and K compounds are easily transported by farmland drainage and surface water to valuable water resources resulting in the deterioration of water quality that warrants the use of novel biosensors to monitor water quality. Recently, it has been proposed that cellular-based biosensor technologies, that is, the bioelectric recognition assay (BERA), utilize live, functional cells in a gel matrix coupled with a sensor system that is able to measure changes in the cellular electric properties. Cells that are able to specifically interact with a target analyte produce a unique pattern of electrical potential as a result of their interaction with this analyte.

Concerning modeling, traditionally, the performance of many bioprocesses has been modeled/predicted using process-based models that are based on mass balance principles, simple reaction kinetics, and a plug flow of water/air stream. An alternate modeling procedure consists of a data driven approach wherein the principles of artificial intelligence (AI) are applied with the help of neural networks The concept of neural network modeling has widespread applications in the fields of applied biosciences and bioengineering.

Understanding Environmental Biotechnology

Environmental biotechnology encompasses a diverse array of techniques and approaches aimed at addressing environmental issues. From wastewater treatment to biofuel production, the applications of environmental biotechnology are wide-ranging and impactful. At its core, environmental biotechnology harnesses the metabolic capabilities of microorganisms, plants, and other living organisms to remediate pollution, restore ecosystems, and create renewable resources.

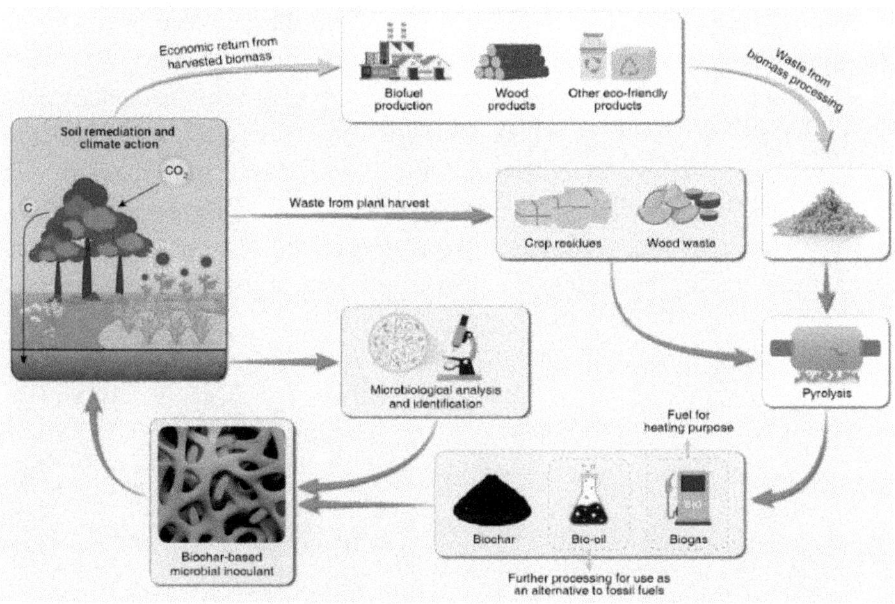

Bioremediation: Cleaning Up Contaminated Environments

One of the most promising applications of environmental biotechnology is bioremediation, the use of living organisms to remove or neutralize pollutants from the environment. Microorganisms such as bacteria and fungi are adept at breaking down a wide range of contaminants, including petroleum hydrocarbons, heavy metals, and industrial chemicals. Through techniques such as bioaugmentation and phytoremediation, scientists are harnessing the power of these natural agents to clean up polluted soils, water bodies, and industrial sites.

Bioenergy: Fuelling a Sustainable Future

As the world seeks alternatives to fossil fuels, bioenergy emerges as a key component of the transition to a sustainable energy future. Environmental biotechnology plays a crucial role in the production of biofuels such as biodiesel, bioethanol, and biogas. Microorganisms such as algae and bacteria can convert organic matter into energy-rich compounds through processes like fermentation and anaerobic digestion. By tapping into the renewable energy potential of biomass, environmental biotechnology offers a viable alternative to carbon-intensive fuels and helps mitigate greenhouse gas emissions.

Biological Waste Treatment: Turning Trash into Treasure

Waste management is a pressing issue in the modern world, with landfills overflowing and oceans choked with plastic pollution. Environmental biotechnology offers innovative solutions for treating and recycling various types of waste. Microbial processes such as composting and anaerobic digestion can convert organic waste into nutrient-rich compost and biogas, reducing the burden on landfills and lowering methane emissions. Meanwhile, advances in bioplastics and biodegradable materials hold promise for reducing the environmental impact of plastics and packaging.

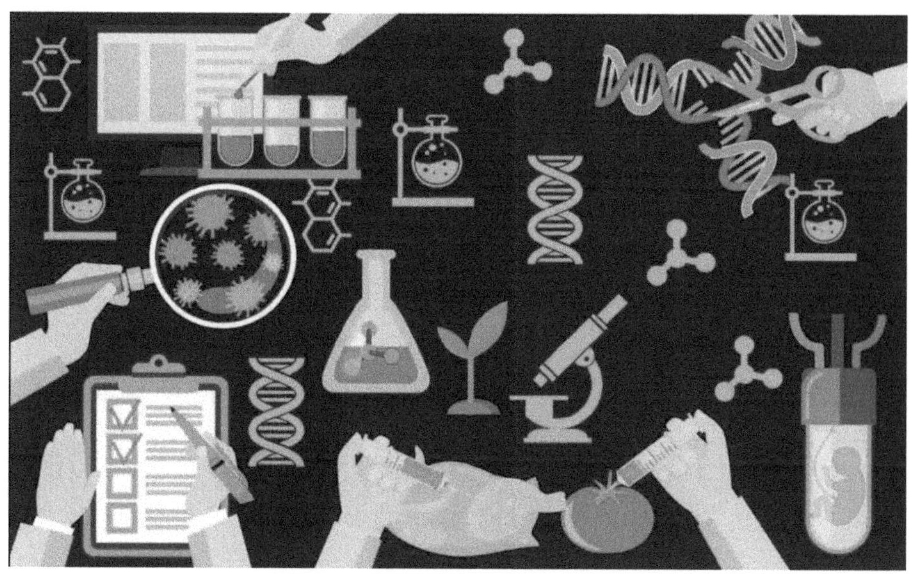

Conclusion: Towards a Greener Tomorrow

As we stand at the crossroads of environmental crisis and technological innovation, environmental biotechnology offers a ray of hope for a sustainable future. By harnessing the power of nature's engineers—microorganisms, plants, and ecosystems—we can address pressing environmental challenges and build a more resilient planet. Through continued research, innovation, and collaboration, we can unlock the full potential of environmental biotechnology and pave the way towards a greener, more sustainable tomorrow.

In the grand tapestry of life on Earth, environmental biotechnology represents a thread of resilience and renewal, weaving together the intricate patterns of nature's design. As stewards of this planet, it is our responsibility to nurture and protect this invaluable resource, ensuring that future generations inherit a world teeming with life and possibility.

REFERENCES

Environ Sci Pollut Res Int. 2008 Jul;15(5):363-93. doi: 10.1007/s11356-008-0024-1. Epub 2008 Jul 3.PMID: 18597132 .

Adv Biochem Eng Biotechnol. 2019;166:373-410. doi: 10.1007/10_2016_73.PMID: 28265703 .

Environ Sci Pollut Res Int. 2008 Jul;15(5):363-93. doi: 10.1007/s11356-008-0024-1. Epub 2008 Jul 3.PMID: 18597132 .

CHAPTER NINE

NANO-HORIZONS: EXPLORING BIOTECHNOLOGY AT THE NANO-SCALE.

Introduction to Nano-biotechnology:

Nanobiotechnology is an interdisciplinary field that encompasses the applications of nanomaterials in biotechnology. This field has significant applications in medicine, health, imaging, immunoproteomics, drug delivery, tissue engineering, cosmetics, agriculture, and pharmacy. Nanobiotechnology has been instrumental in developing intelligent drug delivery and gene therapy tools, nanobiosensors, nanodiagnostics, nanobioconstructs, nanofluidic devices, and bio-compatible nanodevices. Nanoparticles nanomaterials, and nanocolloids can be synthesized by using biological, chemical, and physical methods. Currently, there is an impending need for the development of cost-effective and environment-friendly methods for the synthesis of biocompatible nanoparticles. In the present chapter, we have attempted to present an overview of the different methods for the synthesis of nanoparticles, the underlying mechanisms of biological synthesis, and the recent trends in their applications in nanobiotechnology.

As nano-scale materials, tools, and methods are used in biological and biomedical processes, nano-biotechnology is the meeting point of nanotechnology and biotechnology. Fundamentally, nano-biotechnology uses the special qualities of nano-materials to modify and engage molecular and cellular biological processes.

Nano-biotechnology is important in many areas, such as energy, environmental science, agriculture, and health, and it presents previously unheard-of chances for innovation and progress:

Medicine: Nano-biotechnology has great potential to transform medication delivery, imaging, treatment, and diagnostics. Targeted delivery of treatments to certain cells or tissues is made possible by nanoparticles, nano-sensors, and nano-devices, which maximizes efficacy while reducing negative effects. Furthermore, the creation of extremely sensitive diagnostic instruments for early illness identification and therapy response tracking is made easier by nanotechnology.

Agriculture: Important issues including crop protection, fertilizer management, and soil health might be resolved by nano-biotechnology. By precisely and carefully delivering agrochemicals, nano-pesticides and nano-fertilizers can lessen their negative effects on the environment and increase crop productivity. Real-time soil quality and crop health monitoring is made possible by nano-sensors, which promote sustainable farming and efficient farming methods.

Environmental Science: Water treatment, pollution control, and environmental rehabilitation all greatly benefit from nanotechnology. By using techniques including adsorption, catalysis, and filtration, nano-materials are used to remove pollutants from soil, water, and the air. Early environmental hazard identification and mitigation are made possible by the great sensitivity and specificity of environmental pollutant monitoring made possible by nano-scale sensors.

Energy: The development of efficient energy conversion systems, energy storage devices, and renewable energy sources is aided by nano-biotechnology. Batteries, fuel cells, and solar cells all use nano-materials to improve energy conversion efficiency, energy capture, and storage capacity. Furthermore, the creation of robust and lightweight materials for energy-efficient applications in electronics, construction, and transportation is made possible by nanotechnology.

In summary, the topic of nano-biotechnology holds great promise for revolutionizing human health, agriculture, environmental sustainability, and energy security. Nano-biotechnology provides creative answers to difficult problems by fusing biological systems with nano-scale science, opening the door to a more promising and sustainable future.

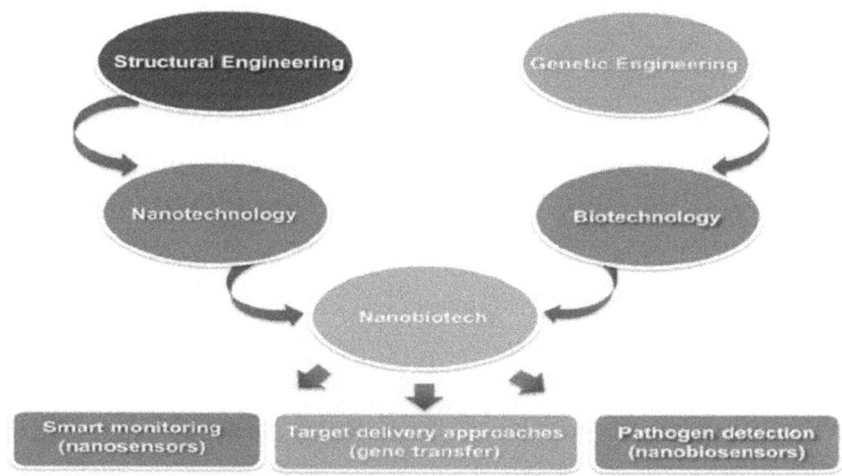

Nano-materials in Biomedical Applications:

With their special qualities and capacities, nanomaterials have become highly useful instruments in biomedical applications, altering a number of areas of healthcare. The following are some applications for various forms of nanomaterials, such as nanoparticles, nanotubes, and nanocomposites:

Drug delivery using nanoparticles: Therapeutic substances can be efficiently transported by nanoparticles, which also shield the pharmaceuticals from deterioration and enable targeted distribution to certain cells or tissues. While regulated release mechanisms guarantee prolonged drug release at the intended location of action, surface modifications allow nanoparticles to elude immune clearance and lengthen their half-life in circulation.

Imaging: Magnetic resonance imaging (MRI), computed tomography (CT), and fluorescence imaging are among the imaging modalities for which nanoparticles are designed to act as contrast agents. Accurate observation of biological structures and disease processes is made possible by functionalization using imaging probes or targeting ligands.

Diagnostics: Pathogens, illnesses, and biomarkers are all detected by integrating nanoparticles into diagnostic tools. Rapid, sensitive, and affordable detection techniques are provided by nanoparticle-based biosensors and assays, allowing for the early identification and monitoring of conditions including cancer, infectious infections, and cardiovascular issues.

Therapeutics: By delivering therapeutic payloads directly to sick cells or tissues, nanoparticles reduce systemic toxicity and enhance treatment results. Functionalized nanoparticles can overcome multidrug resistance mechanisms, carry cytotoxic medications or nucleic acids, and specifically target cancer cells. These properties increase the effectiveness of cancer therapy while lowering adverse effects.

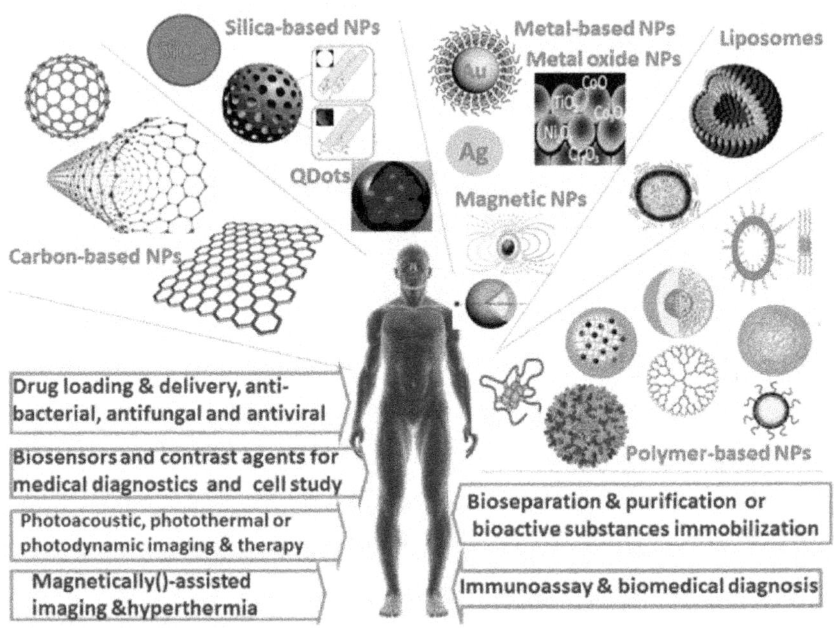

Nanostructures for Tissue Engineering and Regenerative Medicine:

Because nanotechnology makes it possible to create nanostructured scaffolds and matrices that closely resemble the extracellular matrix (ECM) found naturally in tissues and organs, tissue engineering and regenerative medicine have advanced dramatically. These nanostructures provide cells a biomimetic microenvironment that fosters differentiation, adhesion, proliferation, and tissue regeneration. This is the way that nanotechnology is applied in this field:

Ways of Nanofabrication:

Electrospinning: A popular method for creating nanofibrous scaffolds for tissue engineering is electrospinning. Nanofibers of tens to hundreds of nanometers in diameter can be produced by subjecting a polymer solution or melt to an electric field. Electrospun nanofibers' large surface area and porosity imitate the structure of the extracellular matrix (ECM), which promotes cell adhesion, migration, and exchange of nutrients.

Self-assembly: Peptides, proteins, and polymers with self-assembling capabilities can spontaneously form nanostructured scaffolds while maintaining precise control over their composition, mechanical characteristics, and biological activity. These nanostructured materials are perfect for tissue engineering applications because they provide programmable molecular recognition and cellular interactions.

Nanoimprint lithography: Using mechanical deformation or the duplication of a master template, nanoimprint lithography enables the creation of nanoscale features and patterns on surfaces. Using this method, nanostructured surfaces can alter surface chemistry and topographical signals to govern morphology, behavior, and function of cells.

3D bioprinting: This technology allows for the exact deposition of cells, growth factors, and biomaterials to form intricate three-dimensional tissue constructions. It also gives spatial control over the arrangement and dispersion of nanostructures. 3D bioprinting allows for the creation of tissue-engineered constructions with improved biological activity, regeneration potential, and structural integrity by adding nanomaterials to bioinks or supporting matrices.

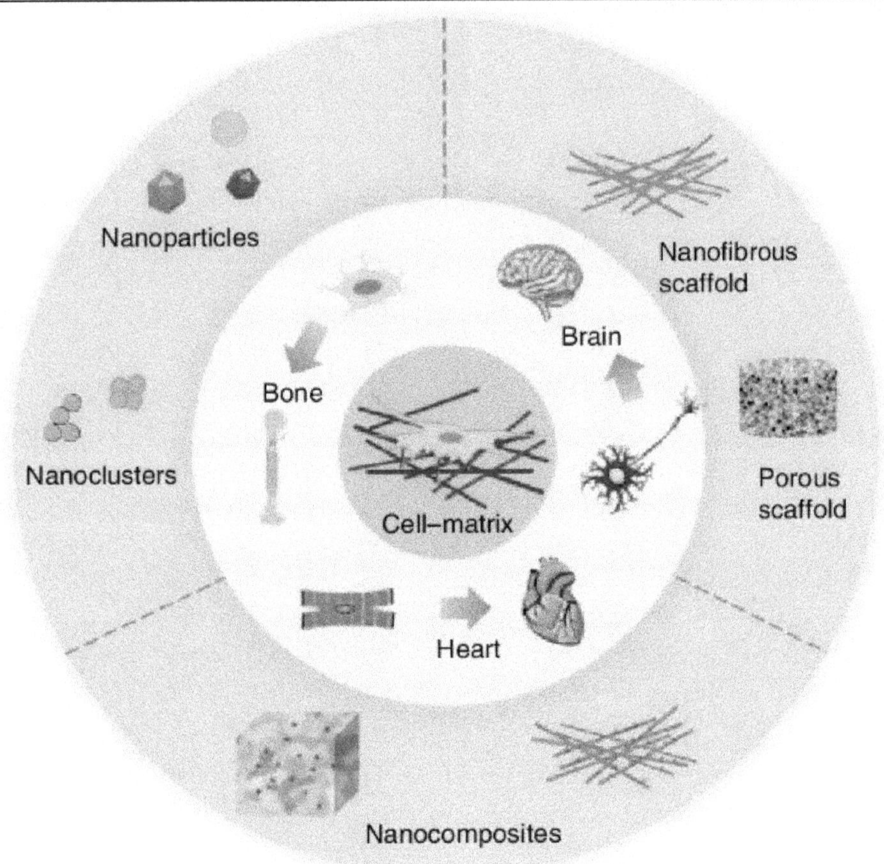

Comparing Bio-functionalization and Functionalization:

Surface modification: To improve cell-material interactions and tissue regeneration, nanotechnology enables the surface modification of scaffolds with bioactive compounds including growth factors, cytokines, and cell adhesion peptides. Additionally, surface functionalization can enhance angiogenesis, provide antimicrobial qualities, and regulate immunological responses, all of which enhance the biocompatibility and functionality of tissue-engineered constructs.

Incorporation of nanoparticles: Scaffold matrices can benefit from the addition of nanoparticles to provide mechanical support, bioactivity, and signaling cues for tissue regeneration. Examples of these nanoparticles include hydroxyapatite, metal, and graphene oxide nanosheets. These nanoparticles can encourage cell adhesion, proliferation, and differentiation by imitating the shape and content of naturally occurring extracellular matrix components.

Drug delivery: To modify cellular behavior and tissue, nanostructured scaffolds can be engineered to distribute bioactive chemicals, medications, or growth factors in a regulated way. Nanocarriers, such as liposomes, micelles, and nanoparticles, can encapsulate therapeutic agents and deliver them locally to the target site, enhancing the efficacy and specificity of regenerative therapies.

Nano-bio catalysts; an attempt to remove the barriers of enzymatic bioprocesses in the biotechnology industry:

Organic enzymes, which are normally found in nature, have large applications in the biotechnology industry. Since organic enzymes are green and eco-friendly, they are usually preferred to commercially synthesized enzymes. Pectinase is considered to be extremely useful for manufacturing purposes. Pectinase application in industrial bioprocesses covers a large range from clarification of juice/ wine and tea/coffee fermentation to wastewater and industrial waste remediation. All enzymes- regardless of being organic or chemically synthesized- consist of limitations that make their usage challenging. Three major disadvantages of enzymes are inefficient recoverability, operational stability, and recyclability (Zhang et al. 2021). Functional nanomaterial-based bio-carriers render a proper environment for the enzymatic immobilization process, therefore facilitating recovery and recycling of enzymes and enhancing the efficiency of bioprocesses in the long run. Accordingly, designing nano-based carriers with these features has been attracted great attention. To achieve this aim, Graphene- immobilized nano-bio-catalysts have been proved to be greatly useful due to the Graphene's characteristics: electrical, optical, thermal, and mechanical high potency (Adeel et al. 2018; Zhang et al. 2021).

Nanomaterial-based nanocatalysts are useful in optimizing the biodiesel production process. This ability is related to the features of nano-scaled materials, including crystallisability, high adsorption and storage potential, having catalytic activities, and great stability and durability. Various materials can be used to create nanoparticles for this mean; some examples are metal oxide (calcium, magnesium oxide, and strontium oxide), Magnetic material, and Carbon. Carbon-based nanomaterials consist of multiple types, such as carbon nanotubes, carbon nanofibers, graphene oxide, and biochar.

All examples mentioned above have been proved to be highly effective in increasing the efficiency of the biodiesel synthesizing process and reducing the time and cost required for operating the process without utilizing nanotechnology (Nizami and Rehan 2018).

Replacing non-renewable energy sources with renewable ones is a great step in guaranteeing a sustainable future. Various devices, including solar and fuel cells, have been developed for this purpose. Conventional fuel cells are made from metal reactants instead of fossil fuels. They provide an electron circulation, transfer electrons from the substrate to specific electrodes, and eventually produce sustainable energy. The metals used as catalysts in fuel cells (e.g., hydrogen, methane, and methanol) are usually expensive and non-durable. On the other hand, biofuel cells use cost-effective bio-catalysts (e.g., microbes and enzymes) instead of metal catalysts. Despite the mentioned advantages, biofuel cells have one major limitation: the low rate of electron transfer between substrate and electrodes, which is significantly enhanced by supplementing biofuel cells with nanomaterials. Nanomaterials are able to assemble the substrate (e.g., enzymes) with the electrodes. In other words, using them in the structure of electrodes, the electron absorption of electrodes improves- related to the high surface area rate of nanomaterials- therefore, a direct transition of electrons between enzymes and electrodes develops. Silver nanoparticles-Graphene oxide (Ag-GO), Graphite, Carbon-nanotube forest (CNTF), Carbon nanotube (CNT), and Nitrogen-doped hollow nanospheres with large pores (pNHCSs) are the nanomaterials applied in nano- biofuel cells. Respectively, Glucose oxidase (GO_x), Glucose oxidase and Laccase, Fructose dehydrogenase & laccase, Glucose oxidase and laccase, and NADH dehydrogenase form the enzymatic system of each nanomaterial (Sharma et al. 2021).

MOFs-based nanozymes:

Nanozymes are classified into two types: (1) natural enzymes that are incorporated with nanomaterials and (2) nanomaterials that exhibit inherent enzymatic features. Exploiting MOFs as nanomaterials in nanozyme structures will produce an emergent form of nanozymes, called: "MOF-based nanozymes"; which have multiple advantages over conventional forms. MOFs provide more catalytic sites, simplify the entrance of small substrate molecules -due to their porous structure-, enhance the substrate exclusivity, and altogether improve the catalytic function of enzymes. MOF-based nanozymes are effective in designing biosensors, biocatalysis, and biomedical imaging techniques. A recent promising application of them is in cancer therapy which reduces side effects significantly (Ding et al. 2020).

Agricultural usages of nanobiotechnology:

Applying nanobiotechnology in agriculture to improve the agricultural production rate has been of great importance recently. Achieving this purpose will solve several problems related to the universal hunger dilemma. Several nanofertilizers, nano pesticides, and nano-bio sensors have been created, which are able to increase crop value and decrease crop loss caused by agricultural pests (Usman et al. 2020). Conventional chemical pesticides and fertilizers can be deteriorative for soil composition and fertility. This happens because chemical residues can target many molecules other than the ones that have been defined as their main targets (Chhipa 2019). Besides, pesticides can have ruinous impacts on the microorganisms that naturally exist in the environment and are required for the crop's growth (Nehra et al. 2021). Utilizing nanoparticles can considerably reduce such unwanted events due to the high exclusivity of these particles. Silver, zinc, iron, titanium, phosphorus, molybdenum, and polymer are suitable materials to be used in the structure of agricultural nanoparticles (Chhipa 2019). Nanoparticles containing nutrients, fertilizers, and pesticides, can be sprayed externally to the plant. The folium will adsorb the nanoparticles and send them to the soil (Chugh et al. 2021).

Another application of nanobiotechnology in diminishing the damages of some traditional pesticides is designing nano-bio sensors that can efficiently detect toxic pesticides. Dichlorvos is one of these toxic pesticides that accumulate in the air, soil, water, and crops; and therefore causes neural, genetical, respirational, and muscular disorders. Dichlorvos-sensitive Nano-biosensors comprise immobilized enzymes embedded in nanomaterials. Acetylcholinesterase (AChE), tyrosinase enzymes, and some others are options for the enzymatic part of the nanodevice. For the nano- matrix section, both organic (carbon, graphene, chitosan, and onion membrane) and inorganic (silver, gold, silica, and Titania) options are available (Mishra et al. 2021). Nanomaterials can enhance the remediation process of contaminated soils through distinct abiotic and biotic directions, including the nano-bioremediation process (Usman et al. 2020).

Other than improving the functions of existed plants, the possibility of introducing engineered plants with better performances has been discussed recently. The term "plant nano bionics" refers to a pioneering idea of involving nanoparticles in living plants to make their intrinsic functions adjustable. The landscape of this idea is designing engineered artificial photosynthetic systems, enhancing the growth rate of this new type of plant, and many other novel applications which are expected to grow extremely in the years ahead (Marchiol 2018).

It is necessary to mention that inorganic nanoparticles that may be found in consumer products, may alter the gut composition and could lead to various gut-related diseases. Thus, there have to be some limitations in nanoparticle agricultural usages (Gangadoo et al. 2021; Ghebretatios et al. 2021).

Nano-bioremediation:

One green and cost-effective approach for treating the pollutant soils to reduce their toxicity is applying living organisms (bacteria, fungi, plants, etc.) through a process named: "bioremediation." Integrating bioremediation with nanoparticles increases the efficiency of the process (Usman et al. 2020). The technology of nano-remediation is a sustainable method to reduce the contaminants of the soil by various means (Yue et al.2021; Sajjadi et al. 2021; Lian et al. 2021). As an example, the reduction of Cr (VI) levels using this technology is known to be worthwhile in many aspects (Azeez et al. 2020; He et al. 2020). Chemically active nanoparticles can trigger the dechlorination/dehalogenation process in organic pollutants and neutralize them, consequently. Even the toughest pollutants are targeted in this nano-bio-based remediation method. The time needed for the purgation of highly contaminated soils will be minimized by virtue of the mentioned technique (Usman et al. 2020). Iron oxide nanoparticles (NP) and Fe3O4/biochar nanocomposites are vastly exploited in the synthesis of nanoparticles of nano-bioremediation (Patra Shahi et al. 2021). It is worth noting that nano zerovalent iron (nZVI) is an effective technology in the case of remediation that has been applied broadly in recent years due to high levels of reactivity for contaminants (Luo et al. 2021; Visentin et al. 2020; Ken and Sinha 2020; Hou et al. 2019; Zhu et al. 2019).

The bioremediation process can be used in water purification as well. Separating solid components from liquid waste is a necessary stage in the water remediation process. The fresh market waste may contain infectious components, which can seriously harm humans and plants. Hence, it is important to develop methods to collect, separate, and treat these adverse agents. Solid wastes in the wastewater contain high amounts of carbohydrates and proteins, and they provide matrices for the colonization of infectious organisms. Altogether, the presence of solid wastes improves the growth rate of pathogenic organisms. After solid matters got collected, they should be stored and treated immediately. The treatment process must not be delayed because the enriched environment of the solid wastes can easily get corrupted. One way to treat them is through triggering the fermentation and composting processes. Adding effective microorganisms (EM), such as lactic acid/phototropic bacteria and yeast, accelerates the conventional fermentation and composting processes used for the solid waste treatment (Al-Gheethi et al. 2020). Costa et al. have sequenced the whole genome of the strain Streptomyces sp. Z38, and detected growth-promoting, heavy metal-eliminating, and anti-microbial features within specific biosynthetic genes. Streptomyces sp. Z38 seems to be a suitable agent for bioremediation due to its ability to decompose heavy metals such as Cr (VI) and Cd (II). Costa et al. have supplemented the bioactive water (BW) extracted from Streptomyces sp. Z38 with AgNO3 additives and produced silver nanoparticles (AgNPs) that are capable of performing the bioremediation process (Costa et al. 2020). There are other effective nanomaterials exploited to reduce many pollutants from soil and wastewater. For instance, utilization of nano-manganese oxide to eliminate ZnII/CoII from water (Mahmoud et al. 2020), application of nano-semiconductors on water and their Photocatalytic effectiveness (Oliveira et al. 2021), nano-scaled Iron (II) sulfide exploited to reduce hexavalent chromium from soil (Tan et al. 2020), production of nanocomposite for eliminating viruses (Al-Attabi et al. 2019), and successful application of nano biosurfactants which cause no toxicity for the environment (Debnath et al. 2021). Nano-bioremediation as an emergent approach causes some concerns and benefits at the same time. It is possible that nanomaterials exploited in this method would be a threat to the organism populations that exist naturally in water bodies. On the other hand, new living organisms would be introduced through bioremediation. The mentioned two scenarios can potentially put the anthropogenic features of ecosystems in danger

(Weijie et al. 2020). Concerning this problem, however, scientists are trying to apply new methods to remove nanoparticles from marine ecosystems via other technologies (Ebrahimbabaie et al. 2020).

Conclusion:

Combining diverse fields of science in a manner that they overcome each other's deficiencies indicates promising results. Within the last decades, biotechnology has made a lot of progress. Merging nanotechnology with biotechnological methods enables scientists to design less time taking, more economical, and more efficient techniques. This Nano-biotechnological approach influences multiple therapeutic, agricultural, environmental, and industrial methods. For instance, the effectiveness of the emergent crisper/cas9 systems increases noticeably by applying the nano-scaled additives at the process.

In this chapter, we investigated the current advancements and limitations of biotechnology, along with the nano-based alternatives rendered by nanotechnology. It seems highly probable that biotechnology will accomplish even more improvements in the future, and its incorporation with nanotechnology gets humankind one step closer to a sustainable future. Besides, the nano-based techniques are less costly compared to the conventional ones. Thus, with nano-biotechnology promoting, a revolution in the economic situation of the world is not implausible.

References:

Abass OK, Zhang K. Nano-Fe mediated treatment of real hydraulic fracturing flowback and its practical implication on membrane fouling in tandem anaerobic-oxic membrane bioreactor. *J Hazard Mater.* 2020;395:122666.

Afra M, Peyghambarzadeh SM, Shahbazi K, Tahmassebi N. Thermo-economic optimization of steam injection operation in enhanced oil recovery (EOR) using nano-thermal insulation. *Energy.* 2021;226:120409.

AlNadhari S, Al-Enazi NM, Alshehrei F, Ameen F. A review on biogenic synthesis of metal nanoparticles using marine algae and its applications. *Environ Res.* 2021;194:110672

Bayda S, Adeel M, Tuccinardi T, Cordani M, Rizzolio F. The history of nanoscience and nanotechnology: from chemical–physical applications to nanomedicine. *Molecules.* 2020;25(1):112.

Benrabah L, Kemel K, Twarog C, Huang N, Solgadi A, Laugel C, Faivre V. Lipid-based Janus nanoparticles for pharmaceutical and cosmetic applications: kinetics and mechanisms of destabilization with time and temperature. *Colloids Surfaces B.* 2020;195:111242.

Ebrahimbabaie P, Meeinkuirt W, Pichtel J. Phytoremediation of engineered nanoparticles using aquatic plants: mechanisms and practical feasibility. J Environ Sci. 2020;93:151–163.

Evelyn Roopngam P. Liposome and polymer-based nanomaterials for vaccine applications. Nanomed J. 2019;6(1):1–10.

Farrera C, Torres Andón F, Feliu N. Carbon nanotubes as optical sensors in biomedicine. ACS Nano. 2017;11(11):10637–10643.

Fidoski J, Benedetti A, Kirkov A, Iliev A, Stamatoski A, Baftijari D. Nano-emulsion complex (propolis and vitamin C) promotes wound healing in the oral mucosa. Oral Maxillofac Patho J. 2020;11(1):1–5.

Fouad GI. A proposed insight into the anti-viral potential of metallic nanoparticles against novel coronavirus disease-19 (COVID-19) Bull Natl Res Cent. 2021;45(1):1–22.

Furtado D, Björnmalm M, Ayton S, Bush AI, Kempe K, Caruso F. Overcoming the blood–brain barrier: the role of nanomaterials in treating neurological diseases. Adv Mater. 2018;30(46):1801362.

Gangadoo S, Nguyen H, Rajapaksha P, Zreiqat H, Latham K, Cozzolino D, Truong VK. Inorganic nanoparticles as food additives and their influence on the human gut microbiota. Environ Sci Nano. 2021;8:1500–1518.

Ghebretatios M, Schaly S, Prakash S. Nanoparticles in the food industry and their impact on human gut microbiome and diseases. Int J Mol Sci. 2021;22(4):1942.

Gökçe D. Influences of nanoparticles on aquatic organisms: current situation of nanoparticles effects in aquatic ecosystems. Sust Eng Innov. 2021;3(1):54–60.

Gong X, Meng Y, Zhu J, Wang X, Lu J, Cheng Y, Tao Y, Wang H. Construct a stable super-hydrophobic surface through acetonitrile extracted lignin and nano-silica and its application in oil-water separation. Ind Crops Prod. 2021;166:113471.

González-Ballesteros N, Prado-López S, Rodríguez-González J, Lastra M, Rodríguez-Argüelles M. Green synthesis of gold nanoparticles using brown algae Cystoseira baccata: Its activity in colon cancer cells. Colloids Surf B. 2017;153:190–198.

Goracci M, Pignochino Y, Marchiò S. Phage display-based nanotechnology applications in cancer immunotherapy. Molecules. 2020;25(4):843.

Goyal S, Joshi P, Singh R. Applications and role of Nano-Silica particles on altering the properties and their usage for oil well cementing. Mater Today Proc. 2021;46:10681–10686.

Hadidi M, Motamedzadegan A, Jelyani AZ, Khashadeh S. Nanoencapsulation of hyssop essential oil in chitosan-pea protein isolate nano-complex. LWT. 2021;144:111254.

Hager S, Fittler FJ, Wagner E, Bros M. Nucleic acid-based approaches for tumor therapy. Cells. 2020;9(9):2061.

Hajiabadi SH, Aghaei H, Kalateh-Aghamohammadi M, Shorgasthi M. An overview on the significance of carbon-based nanomaterials in upstream oil and gas industry. J Pet Sci Eng. 2020;186:106783.

He Y, Lin H, Luo M, Liu J, Dong Y, Li B. Highly efficient remediation of groundwater co-contaminated with Cr (VI) and nitrate by using nano-Fe/Pd bimetal-loaded zeolite: process product and interaction mechanism. Environ Pollut. 2020;263:114479.

FRONTIERS BEYOND EARTH: BIOTECHNOLOGY IN SPACE EXPLORATION

INTRODUCTION:

From the dawn of civilization, humanity has been captivated by the cosmos. The twinkling stars above have inspired myths, legends, and scientific inquiry, driving us to explore the vast unknown. With technological advancements, the dream of space exploration has evolved from ancient celestial observations to modern-day missions reaching the farthest reaches of our solar system and beyond. The Space Age, ignited by the launch of Sputnik 1 in 1957, ushered in an era of unprecedented discovery and achievement. From the Apollo moon landings to the robotic explorations of Mars and the outer planets, human ingenuity has pushed the boundaries of space exploration, revealing the wonders of the universe and expanding our understanding of our place within it.

In the vast expanse of space, where resources are scarce and the environment harsh, humanity's quest for exploration and colonization relies heavily on innovation and adaptation. Among the myriad technologies at our disposal, biotechnology stands out as a pivotal tool in our journey beyond Earth's confines. Its applications in space exploration are multifaceted, ranging from sustaining life in the unforgiving vacuum of space to laying the groundwork for sustainable habitats on distant celestial bodies.

At the forefront of biotechnological innovation in space exploration is the concept of bioregenerative life support systems (BLSS). These systems mimic Earth's natural ecosystems by utilizing biological processes to recycle waste products, generate oxygen, and produce food. In the microgravity environment of space, where resources are limited and every ounce of cargo comes at a premium, BLSS offer a sustainable solution for long-duration missions. By harnessing the power of photosynthesis and microbial metabolism, these systems can create closed-loop environments capable of supporting human life independent of resupply missions from Earth.

One of the cornerstones of BLSS is space agriculture, which involves cultivating plants in space habitats to provide astronauts with fresh food and oxygen. Through the use of hydroponic or aeroponic systems, researchers have successfully grown a variety of crops onboard spacecraft and space stations. Beyond merely supplementing astronauts' diets, space agriculture plays a crucial role in maintaining psychological well-being during extended missions, offering a connection to nature and a sense of normalcy amidst the sterile confines of space.

However, the challenges of cultivating plants in microgravity are manifold, requiring innovative solutions to overcome issues such as water distribution, nutrient absorption, and the absence of gravity-driven processes like root growth. Biotechnological advancements, such as genetic engineering and synthetic biology, hold the promise of tailor-made crops optimized for space conditions, capable of thriving in the absence of gravity and resisting the stresses of cosmic radiation.

Furthermore, biotechnology plays a pivotal role in biomanufacturing in microgravity environments, offering the potential to produce pharmaceuticals, biomaterials, and biofuels with greater efficiency and purity than terrestrial methods. The unique properties of microgravity, such as reduced fluid shear and convection, can lead to improved yields and product quality in bioreactor-based manufacturing processes. Additionally, the space environment presents opportunities for novel biotechnological applications, such as the production of exotic materials in the vacuum of space or the development of bio-inspired materials inspired by the extreme conditions found beyond Earth's atmosphere.

Space bioprocess engineering (SBE) is an emerging multi-disciplinary field to design, realize, and manage biologically-driven technologies specifically with the goal of supporting life on long term space missions. SBE considers synthetic biology and bioprocess engineering under the extreme constraints of the conditions of space. A coherent strategy for the long term development of this field is lacking.

Astrobiotech for space exploration:

It is possible to identify some fields related to space exploration in which modern biotechnology techniques play a key role.

One example is biomedical studies to control and reduce space-related stressors on living systems in order to assist space exploration. Since space is a harmful environment for terrestrial life, is it necessary to develop techniques that are able to reduce space-related stressors such as microgravity, radiation, isolation, and confinement. In order to develop these techniques, a deep understanding of the biological mechanisms that underlie the disruption of organismal, tissue, and cellular homeostasis is required. Numerous experiments concerning different biological systems have been performed, both ground-based and in space. As far as in-space research is concerned, modern biotechnology is able to deliver instrument miniaturization and real-time data analysis, two aspects that are crucial in space as space and weight are limited and spacecraft re-entry to Earth is detrimental for biological-sample integrity. (Karouia et al, 2017)

Another topic is biology for life support (such as the "MEliSSA" project) and in-situ resource utilization. These techniques will use microorganism populations re-engineered to execute particular functions. These biological systems have to be validated, including being monitored during the whole mission to assess their performance, stability, and high-throughput to provide reliable information in a brief amount of time.

Sensitive techniques such as PCR, gene expression, or proteomics measurements are able to identify and to monitor potential terrestrial biological contaminants for any mission aimed at the search for life. This is important for planetary protection, but also for basic astrobiology research, to study the limits of life in space, and possible evolution in other environments.

Biotechnological development of plants for Space Agriculture:

If humankind is ever to undertake long-term space missions and colonization, establishing an efficient space farming system would be essential for human survival in space. However, existing crops are not sufficiently cost effective and productive for use on space farms. Hence, we propose a Whole-Body Edible and Elite Plant (WBEEP) strategy for space crop improvement. Relying on plant biotechnology, the WBEEP strategy aims to develop crops with more edible parts, richer nutrient content, higher yields, and higher mineral nutrient use efficiencies for space farms.

Potato (Solanum tuberosum L.) is believed to be one of the top contenders for space agriculture due to the following advantages: (1) high harvest index and tuber yield and carbohydrate-rich tubers that can provide a large amount of energy for humans; (2) simple horticultural and food processing requirements; and (3) high tolerance against stresses with the ability to develop normally during spaceflight1. Importantly, potatoes can be asexually propagated through tubers and sexually propagated through seeds. Asexual reproduction can ensure the regeneration of food resources and stable nutritional value, while sexual reproduction can guarantee a higher propagation coefficient and lower storage and transportation costs. However, potatoes cannot be efficiently cultivated in space until inherent defects related to their high solanine content, low yield and nutrient accumulation, and low fertilizer use efficiency are overcome.

Research applications of astrobiotech:

Modern biotechnology allows high-throughput "omics" technologies for analysis of biological samples. These techniques span across genomics, transcriptomics, proteomics, and metabolomics.

High-throughput biotechnology techniques allow researchers, technicians, and aerospace operators to carry out measurements in-situ, overcoming the limitations of post-flight sample analysis. This provides several advantages, such as the possibility of real-time monitoring of the biological environment and increased accuracy of the sampled data.

Research and development of space biotechnology is highly expensive. Therefore, it is necessary to identify those technologies that are the most valuable and offer the best cost-benefit relationship.

As an example, the Columbus laboratory is the European Space Agency's largest single contribution to the ISS and the first permanent European research facility in space. The research projects that can be performed concern several scientific topics, among which are astrobiology and space physiology. Biolab, one of the five internal payloads of the Columbus Module, supports biological experiments on micro-organisms, cells, tissue cultures, small plants and small invertebrates.

Microbial Detection in Air System for Space (MiDASS) is an instrument being developed by ESA and bioMérieux S.A. for in-situ detection of microbial contamination. This system allows pathogen detection on air, surface, and water samples taken on the spacecraft. This instrument is made of two sections, one for automated sample preparation and the other for amplification and in situ detection of bacterial and fungal contaminants. It is based on real-time nucleic acid sequence-based amplification and molecular beacon detection technology.

Another experiment, WetLab-2, allows quantitative gene expression analysis via RT-qPCR. This new NASA initiative is made to perform on-orbit analysis of samples from many organisms, including humans.

The potential of astrobiotech:

Space biotechnology is a field aimed at applying tools of modern biology to advance space exploration. Astrobiotechnology is focused on identifying technology gaps for longer missions and to transition methodologies and technologies from Earth-based experiments to other planets, highlighting instrument technologies and sample handling.

Future long-term missions in space will require a significant amount of food, water, and oxygen in order to respond to the crew's necessities. For a Mars mission, it would be approximately 30 tons, a quantity of mass not supported by the available launch systems. Besides, each kilogram of food launched to the International Space Station costs about $10,000. The final goal is to be completely independent without relying on any supplies from Earth, and biotechnology is the solution to satisfy the needs of long-term space missions.

Limitations and considerations:

Research and development of space biotechnology is highly expensive. Therefore, it is necessary to identify those technologies that are the most valuable and offer the best cost-benefit relationship. For example, 3D-printing might enable astronauts to produce a wide variety of tools and even biological materials such as human tissue on board. However, the main advances rely on the "omics" techniques: amplification and sequencing of DNA as well as measuring levels of RNA transcripts, proteins, and metabolites in a cell. The development of in-situ data analysis capabilities is an alternative to the traditional paradigm of post-flight analysis, which offers advantages such as reduced concerns about sample integrity, because is not necessary to bring samples back to Earth. However, not all data can be analyzed on board.

Recent years have seen several applications of biotechnology in space. Genetic engineering technology is already being used in order to grow plants to ensure food supply. "MELiSSA" is an implemented life support system that is designed to permit the recycling of approximately 100% of the wastes. These benefits are also not limited to space exploration. Pharmaceutical and biotechnology companies are using the US ISS National Laboratory to conduct experiments regarding protein crystallization to develop immunotherapy drugs and to test new technologies for assessing cellular function to improve evaluation of drug effectiveness and safety.

Astrobiotech in Europe:

There is an interest in astrobiotechnology in Europe. The Horizon 2020 program aims, in its words, to "foster a cost-effective and innovative Space industry and research community." EU policy and societal needs are expected to be addressed through space sector advances. Astrobiotechnology belongs to this scheme and relevant projects will be accordingly funded as long as they comply with such needs. According to official EU sources, 30 million euros were available back in 2014–2015 in the frame of Horizon funding. Moreover, astrobiotechnology is supported by ESA Business Application, a scheme in which ESA offers financial assistance, partnership, and technical and commercial guidance to any company or organization residing in ESA member states. Projects may be supported at any stage, from the initial design to their implementation. It appears that initiatives in astrobiotechnology are welcome from any group of people, regardless if it is a renowned company, a startup, a scientific group or a mere NGO, and at any stage.

Providing researchers with the right instruments and capacities paves the way for potential significant discoveries in space biology.

Last but not least, students in EU and ESA member states are encouraged to work on astrobiotechnology as part of their thesis research. ESA has run programs such as "Fly your Thesis," providing young researchers the chance to simulate their experiment in microgravity conditions. Being endorsed by ESA, such initiatives not only receive valuable feedback but are also communicated to industry and stakeholders, promoting collaboration between academia and industry. Although such collaborations are debatable, EU policy-making can guarantee the sustainability of these partnerships and their development in the frame of societal policy and human rights.

The involvement of the EU in promoting biotechnology, and R&D in general, in space is beneficial for the EU itself at the same time. Challenging European policy issues such as the Brexit or the so-called division between the EU North and South countries can be addressed in this context. The contribution of EU institutions to the sector could be an inhibiting factor for Brexit, whereas the equal participation of research groups from Italy, Greece, or Portugal and Germany or Denmark inspires mutual respect to the scientific communities of member states. In a broader sense, providing that the collaboration for SRE is expanded to partner states to the EU, the integration of Eastern Europe, Mediterranean partners, and Western Balkans to the EU can be literally skyrocketed.

Conclusion:

The investment in space biotechnology will require facilities for long-term, controlled culture growth and for storing samples. Providing researchers with the right instruments and capacities paves the way for potential significant discoveries in space biology. It may lead to not only to the engineering of novel microorganisms that will be able to survive in harsh conditions and generate or reprocess valuable resources, but also fundamental progress in space medicine to protect astronauts from diseases and mitigate the effects of space-related stressors; advances that could be useful also on Earth.

References:

NASA Astrobiology Institute (July 24, 2018), Introduction and Overview, Retrieved on September 20, 2019.

Space Station Research Explorer on NASA.gov Research Database (n.d.), "Biotechnology and Biology" Section, Retrieved on September 20, 2019.

Steele, A. & Toporski, J, Astrobiotechnology, Proceedings of the First European Workshop on Exo-Astrobiology, 16–19 September 2002, Graz, Austria. Ed.: Huguette Lacoste. ESA SP-518, Noordwijk, Netherlands: ESA Publications Division, ISBN 92-9092-828-X, 2002, p. 235–238.

Karouia, F., Peyvan, K. & Pohorille, A. (2017) Towards biotechnology in space: High-throughput instruments for in situ biological research beyond Earth. Biotechnol. Adv. 35, 905–932.

Columbus laboratory / Columbus / Human and Robotic Exploration / Our Activities / ESA. (2019) Retrieved September 25, 2019.

Biolab / Columbus / Human and Robotic Exploration / Our Activities / ESA. (n.d.) Retrieved on September 25, 2019.

Astrobiotechnology, Biomimicry, Biodesign, Biodigital, (n.d.), Retrieved on September 20, 2019.

Fernández, C. (2019). To Reach Mars, We Need Biotechnology. Retrieved September 23. 2019.

NASA Astrobiology Institute. (2019). Retrieved September 20, 2019.

US ISS National Laboratory, (2019), Continuing Innovations In Life Sciences Research on the Space Station, Retrieved September 17, 2019.

European Commission, Horizon 2020, (2019), Space, Retrieved September 20, 2019.

European Space Agency, (2019), Space Biotechnology Applications, Accessed on September 25, 2019.

European Space Agency, (n.d.) Fly Your Thesis, Retrieved September 24, 2019.

Sigalas, (2017) European Union Space Policy, Oxford Research Encyclopedia – Politics, Retrieved September 24, 2019.

CHAPTER ELEVEN

BIO-REVOLUTION: NAVIGATING CHALLENGES AND SEIZING OPPORTUNITIES IN BIOTECHNOLOGY

Introduction:-

Among the various new technologies that have emerged during the 1970s, biotechnology has likely received the most attention. Biotechnology has proven capable of creating immense riches and influencing every major sector of the economy. Biotechnology is defined as biology-based technology that uses organisms or their parts to manufacture or modify things, as well as to improve plants, animals, and microbes. Biotechnology is divided into animal, environmental, aquatic, microbiological, medicinal, and forensic categories. Modern biotechnology has promising applications such as environmental protection, criminal isolation, and food and pharmaceuticals production. It has applications in nanotechnology, cloning, gene therapy, recombinant DNA technology, embryonic stem cell research, biofuels, biobanks, and biotechnology sectors. Biotechnology and bioindustries play a crucial role in the knowledge-based economy by advancing life sciences, applied sciences, and related technologies. Today, the international economy has increased significantly due to the implementation of the latest biological technologies

Biotechnology has already had a significant impact on healthcare, food production and processing, agriculture and forestry, environmental protection, and material and chemical manufacturing. Biotechnological innovation is becoming increasingly recognized as a valuable instrument for improving world health. The problem, however, is defining the role of technology transfer in developing medicines for diseases common in underdeveloped countries. Because of the pharmaceutical industry's focus on health areas with the highest profit margins, a significant difference in access to cheap medicines has formed over the last decade between the developed and poor worlds. Genetic engineering, culture of recombinant microorganisms, animal and plant cells, metabolic engineering, hybridoma technology, bioelectronics, nanobiotechnology, protein engineering, transgenic animals and plants, tissue and organ engineering, immunological assays, genomics and proteomics, bioseparations, and bioreactor technologies are among the defining technologies of modern biotechnology.

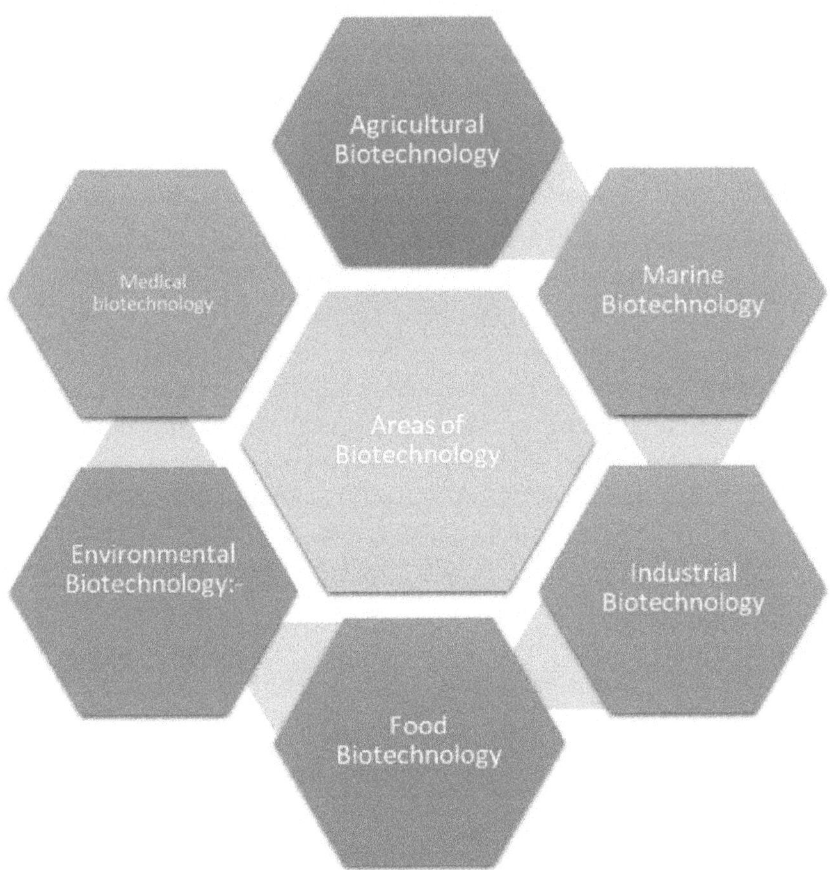

The environmental and economic advantages that biotechnology can provide in manufacturing, monitoring, and waste management are underlined. These advantages include: greatly reduced reliance on nonrenewable fuels and other resources; reduced potential for pollution of industrial processes and products; the ability to safely destroy accumulated pollutants for environmental remediation; improved production economics; and the ability to produce existing and novel products sustainably.Biotechnology breakthroughs are recognized for their potential societal advantages; but, much care must be taken to ensure that modernization efforts prioritize safety and security, as well as the ELSI for how they are generated, transmitted, utilized, disposed of, and managed. For example, in 2018, a biotechnology experiment resulted in the birth of twin girls who were believed to be HIV-free after embryos were manipulated with CRISPR—clustered regularly interspaced short palindromic repeats, a gene editing method. This single example, its process, and its findings open a "Pandora's Box" of issues and dilemmas about biotechnology misuse.

The potential applications of CRISPR and other genomic editing tools highlight the importance of developing and coordinating biotechnology frameworks that prioritize and synthesize non-technical demands within typical R&D pipelines. Biotechnology combines science and engineering to process materials through biological agents. Biological agents including enzymes, plant cells, and microbes are utilized to Produce medications, foods, and biochemicals for warfare. Biotechnology was founded on the discovery of DNA structure in the early 1950s. The hereditary material is deoxyribonucleic acid (DNA), which carries all of the information that governs every aspect of a person's existence. DNA is made up of deoxyribose, phosphate, and four nitrogenous bases. The base and sugar combine to produce nucleoside, while the base, sugar, and phosphate combine to form nucleotide . These are placed on DNA in a specific orientation known as order or sequence, and they include information that allows them to be expressed as proteins. DNA has double helix structure, with two strands being complementary and antiparallel to each other, in which A on one strand base pairs with T, and G base pairs with C contains two and three bonds, respectively. DNA is a lengthy, compact molecule that is neatly wrapped in our nucleus. The DNA is capable of creating additional copies of itself using the information contained in it, such as the order or sequence of nucleotides. This is termed DNA replication.

Louis Pasteur developed vaccinations using biotechnology in the late 1800s. Biotechnology is rapidly evolving and enjoying a second wave of growth. Biotechnology has numerous benefits, including increasing crop output, conserving biodiversity, protecting the environment, reducing soil erosion, improving production stability, and producing high-quality vitamins and proteins. Biotechnology is often associated with medical and agricultural applications that rely on understanding the genetic code of life. Biotechnology began millennia ago when plants and animals were selectively bred and microbes were utilized to produce beer, wine, cheese, and bread. However, the area expanded over time, and it is now defined as the use or manipulation of living organisms to create beneficial compounds for medical, agricultural, and/or industrial applications. Conventional biotechnology is defined as the use of living organisms for specific reasons such as bread/cheese production, whereas current biotechnology is concerned with the utilization of biological molecules such as DNA, monoclonal antibodies, biologics, and so on. Before delving into the technical breakthroughs of DNA and hence recombinant DNA technology, let us have a basic grasp of DNA and its function

2. Clssification:-

The primary subfields of biotechnology include medical (red), agricultural (green), industrial (white), marine (blue), food, and environmental biotechnology(Figure 1).

2.1 Medical biotechnology:-

Medical biotechnology has grown rapidly in recent years, resulting in the creation of a number of novel procedures for illness prevention, diagnosis, and treatment. Novel methodologies, such as polymerase chain reaction, gene sequencing, fluorescence in situ hybridization, microarrays, cell culture, gene silencing using interference RNA, and genome editing, have significantly contributed to the advancement of health science, including the sequencing of the human genome, the use of stem cells for regenerative medicine, tissue engineering, antibiotic development, and the generation of monoclonal antibodies for therapeutic use. Pharmacogenomics examines how an individual's genetics influence their body's response to medications. Gene testing is the direct analysis of the DNA molecule itself..

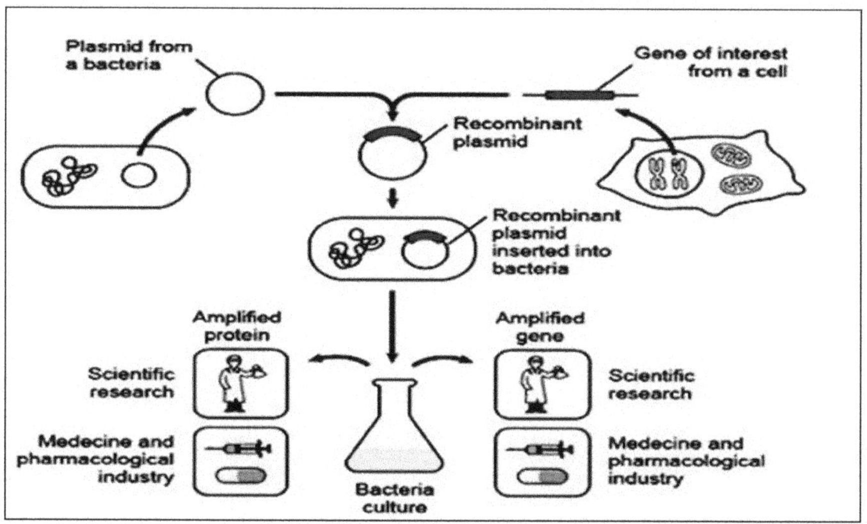

Recombinant DNA (rDNA) technology combines DNA molecules from several sources and inserts them into a host organism to produce goods for human use. The first rDNA molecule was created in 1973 by Paul Berg, Herbert Boyer, Annie Chang, and Stanley Cohen. The discovery of restriction enzymes set the groundwork for rDNA technology, which is now used in modern genetic engineering. Since the COVID-19 pandemic, rDNA technology has broadened the application of medicine and vaccines for humans(Figure 2).

In the creation of recombinant pharmaceuticals, tissue engineering goods, regenerative medicines such as stem cell and gene therapy, and a variety of other biotechnology products to improve people's lives. Biotechnological technologies are used to create purified biotherapeutic drugs on an industrial scale. These contain both novel agents and agents that were previously only available in limited quantities. Crude vaccinations were employed in ancient China, India, and Persia. For ages, the East practiced inoculation with scabs containing the smallpox virus. In 1798, English country doctor Edward Jenner demonstrated that inoculation with pus from lesions caused by a similar cowpox virus could prevent smallpox significantly more safely. It marked the start of vaccination. Humans have profited enormously from the implementation of immunization programs.

2.2 Agricultural Biotechnology:-

Farmers prioritize crop qualities like high yield, disease resistance, insect pest resistance, and high nutrient content, color, texture, and flavor. Agriculture in global strategic restructuring aims to integrate production and use vertically. Genetic engineering is transforming agriculture by allowing for a wider variety of plants and animals. Scientists aim to employ recombinant technology to enhance the productivity of plants and animals used in agriculture, in order to address the issue of human production on the planet(Figure 3).

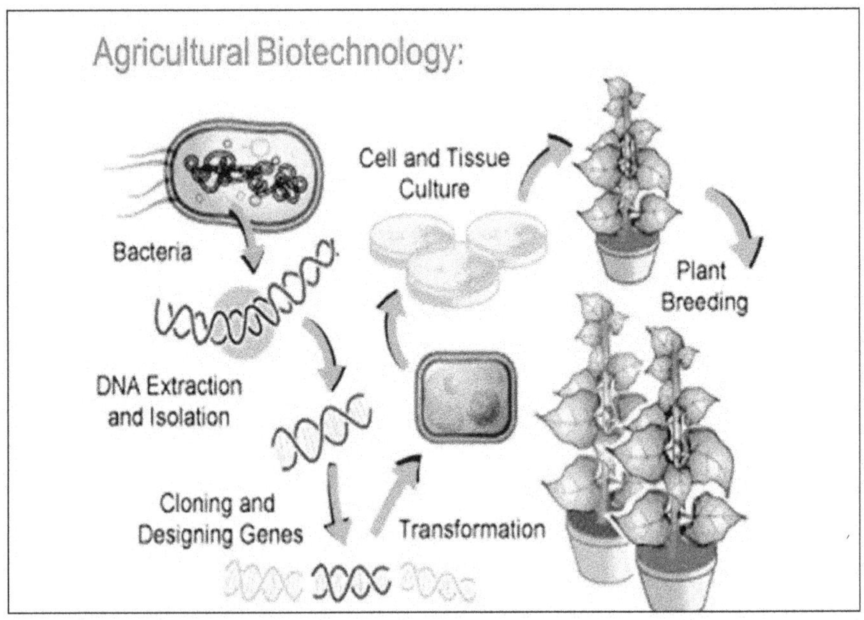

Agricultural biotechnology attempts to bring sustainable farming practices with the highest production potential while having the least negative impact on the environment. Pest control, for example, proved to be a significant difficulty. Thus, the Bt gene, derived from the bacterium Bacillus thuringiensis, serves as an insect-resistant gene when placed into crop plants such as cotton, corn, and soybean, so preventing disease invasion, and the technology is known as integrated pest management. This management is beneficial in decreasing the use of possibly harmful pesticides on the crop. Not only is limited or low pesticide use advantageous for crops, but it also reduces the load of polluting chemicals on the environment significantly.

2.3 Industrial Biotechnology:-

Industrial biotechnology refers to the use of biotechnological tools (bioprocessing) to produce biotechnology-derived goods (fuels, polymers, enzymes, chemicals, and many other compounds) on an industrial scale. The goal is to create innovative industrial manufacturing methods and products that are more cost effective and superior to existing ones while also having a low environmental impact. In industrial biotechnology, microorganisms are being investigated for the production of material goods such as cheese, biorefineries in which oils, sugars, and biomass can be turned into biofuels, bioplastics, and biopolymers and value-added chemicals from biomass. The use of current techniques can increase efficiency and lessen the environmental impact of industrial operations such as textile, paper, pulp, and chemical production. Figure 4 highlights historical developments in industrial biotechnology.

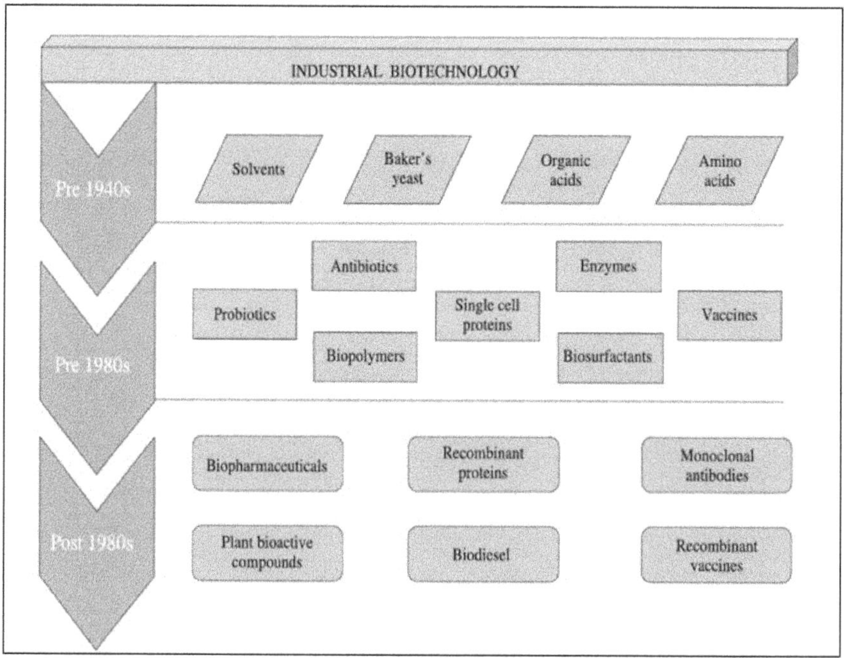

For example, the creation and use of biocatalysts, such as enzymes, to synthesis compounds, as well as the development of antibiotics and better tasting liquors, and their application in the food business, have enabled safe and effective processing for sustainable production. The textile industry uses biotechnological tools to polish textiles and clothing. Biotechnology also creates spider silk and biotech-derived cotton, which is warmer and stronger, with better dye uptake and retention, absorbency, and wrinkle and shrink resistance.

2.4 Marine Biotechnology:-

Marine or aquatic biotechnology, commonly known as "blue biotechnology," is concerned with the exploration and utilization of the world's marine resources. Aquatic or marine life has long piqued people's interest and provided a means of subsistence. Because water covers the majority of the world, oceans and aquatic systems are home to approximately 75-80 percent of all life forms. It can improve aquaculture species' growth rate, reproductive potential, disease resistance, and resistance to severe environmental conditions (e.g., warm and cold water) . Transgenesis, a strategy for enhancing economic qualities such as growth rate, disease resistance, feed conversion, and cold tolerance, is a recent advancement in biotechnology. Over 15 fish species have had successful gene transfers. Aqua Advantage TM is a transgenic salmon fish that grows 4-6 times quicker and uses 20% less food than the control. It was developed in Canada and the United States of America (USA). By understanding ocean geochemical processes, researchers want to address food supply needs, uncover health-benefiting substances, improve sea animal features, and protect marine ecosystems.

2.5 Food Biotechnology:-

Food biotechnology is an emerging topic that has the potential to boost food production while also increasing nutritional content and taste. Food fermentation is the earliest biotechnological technique. It includes food additives, plant and animal cell cultures. New advancements in fermentation and enzyme technologies, genetic advancements in food biotechnology, including protein engineering, bioengineering, and monoclonal antibody techniques, have opened up new possibilities. Traditional agriculture and crop breeding are not considered food biotechnology. However, agricultural biotechnology, including animal and plant foods, is predicted to be a key driver of development in the agri-food business. The food is safe and useful because it requires fewer herbicides and insecticides. The method promises to create foods with more flavors, more vitamins and minerals, and less fat when cooked. Food biotechnology may remove allergies and harmful components from foods, improving their utility.

2.6 Environmental Biotechnology:-

Environmental biotechnology focuses on using biological systems and processes for waste treatment and management. The application of biological bioremediation is using biological processes to remove toxins from the environment. Biodegradation is a natural process, while bioremediation accelerates the decomposition of pollutants such as liquid and solid wastes, contaminated ground water, and toxic goods, resulting in a contaminant-free site region. This method has the potential to treat contaminated soil and groundwater. Plant photosynthesis is a highly efficient biotechnological method for reducing CO_2 emissions.

A biotechnological technique to genetically increase photosynthetic CO_2 fixation is desirable. Plants rely on the enzyme RUBP-case to repair CO_2. Efforts are underway to genetically modify this enzyme in plants to boost photosynthetic efficiency and utilize more CO_2 at once. Biotechnology allows for targeted cleanup of low-level pollutants on-site. Bioremediation may involve the following stages. Examine the contaminated site; The site characterization process involves: Analysis of physical attributes To remediate contaminated soil or water, consider the location, source, nature, distribution, and concentration of contaminants. Additionally, isolate and characterize naturally occurring microorganisms with bioremediation potential. The project involves cultivating viable organisms, evaluating their catabolic capability in contaminated material, monitoring and testing in chemically contaminated media, and implementing bioremediation in the field.

3. Challenges:-

Bioethics is a subfield that addresses ethical issues in the life sciences, assisting individuals in making informed judgments regarding the acceptable applications of biotechnology and biological science. It covers questions regarding theoretical potential, disparities between animal biotechnology products and traditional technologies, environmental risks, animal health and welfare issues, and appropriate policy implications. The government also aims to prohibit embryo use and commercial trafficking of human materials. A survey of moral and ethical sensitivity found that respondents prioritize ethical views in regenerative medicine, distributional fairness in genetically modified food, nanotechnology, and animal cloning, as well as the importance of moral governance over scientific evidence in synthetic biology and animal cloning.

3.1 Ethical and Social Challenges:-

To address biosecurity issues, the Committee on Advances in Technology and the Prevention of Their Application to Next-Generation Bioterrorism and Biological Warfare Threats in the United States suggests that life scientists develop a shared culture of awareness. It underlines the significance of having oversight mechanisms for biological capabilities that may cause harm or have dual use applications. To ensure effective biosecurity governance, stakeholders must foresee future security requirements and limit potential misuse of biotechnology research. Biotechnology should stress four principles: autonomy, nonmaleficence, beneficence, and justice. Equitable biotechnological procedures strive to distribute risks and benefits among the same population. The legal ramifications of biotechnology are ambiguous, as no particular restrictions are in place. However, flexible laws have been enacted to control biological capacities without explicit titles. Developers must comply with area laws and policies, as well as international agreements. Cultural norms and societal taboos shape critical attitudes toward biotechnology. Cultural ideas, social norms, and media frameworks all have a big impact on how the public perceives biotechnology and gene editing. It is critical to recognize and respect the varied risk cultures and moral perspectives on the perceived risks and opportunities of biotechnology.Innovations in industrial biotechnology promote societal themes such as sustainability, naturalness, risk management, innovation trajectories, and economic justice.

3.1.1 Sustainability:-

Industrial biotechnology's sustainability can be assessed through quantifiable factors like CO_2 reduction, resource use, and toxic substance release. Nonquantifiable factors, such as social well-being, are complex and difficult to quantify. Literature on social sustainability for bioeconomy is increasing, discussing issues like employment, working conditions, labor rights, gender equality, social development, and food security. Some aspects of sustainability are ideological and influenced by preferred societal structures and future effects of a specific technology. For example, the vanillin case highlights the importance of preserving local ecosystems and traditional farming practices. However, some oppose genetic engineering due to concerns about economic monopolies and unnecessary risks. A reliable system for sustainability assessment is crucial for industrial biotechnology advancement. Different views on sustainability are important when designing indicators, as they reflect concerns and serve the public good.

3.1.2 Naturalness:-

Sustainability is inextricably tied to the concept of naturalness, which presents two questions: what is natural, and which items can be considered natural and which cannot. Labeling products developed from industrial biotechnology calls into doubt the distinction between natural and engineered products. Differences in values, views, and convictions add to the discussion. Some people regard nature as fragile and should be treated with caution, while others see it as a resource with possible solutions.

3.2 Protecting Human Subjects in Clinical Trials:-

Since 1999, the University of Pennsylvania's gene therapy study has been fraught with controversy due to allegations of ineligibility and a lack of informed consent. This led to heightened scrutiny and the implementation of new standards. Professor Jeremy Sugarman highlights the need of proper research conduct throughout the study cycle, emphasizing that attention to all aspects is critical for the scientific enterprise's success and participant safety.

3.3 Affordability:-

The rising expense of healthcare, particularly prescription costs, has been and will continue to be a political hot potato. Regardless of what the US Food and Drug Administration says or does, a large portion of the public, their federal representatives, and their governors do not appear to believe the pharmaceutical industry's argument that research and development is funded by current prices and that price controls could stifle R&D.

The discussion over the utility of expensive biotech treatments for chronic illnesses is expected to exacerbate ethical problems. After all, a cholesterol tablet could cost $3 each day, totaling over $1,100 per year. Compare that to a biologic that costs $20,000 per year — or even most costly.

3.4 Gene Therapy:-

Some biotech efforts to better health have proven more difficult than others. One example is gene transfer, which involves replacing a faulty gene with a normally functioning one. In most cases, the normal gene is delivered to target tissues using a virus that has been genetically engineered to be harmless. In 1990, the National Institutes of Health (NIH) conducted the first ex vivo gene transfer experiment on Ashanti DeSilva, who had severe combined immunodeficiency (SCID), which helped increase her immune response and successfully cure an enzyme deficiency. However, treatment was needed every several months. However, 9 years later, a severe setback occurred in the gene therapy trial with the death of 18-year-old Jesse Gelsinger suffering from ornithine transcarbamylase (OTC) deficiency owing to intensive inflammatory reactions are followed by gene therapy treatment. There were both favorable and negative experiences with gene therapy experiments, which led to tougher safety regulations in clinical trials.

3.5 Genetically Modified Food:-

Genetically engineered crops with insect resistance genes were planted on billions of acres of land. These crops were quite popular due to their great yield and insect resistance. However, some pests eventually developed resistance to a few of these transgenic crops, providing a resistant pest danger. The other technologies, such as "traitor" and "terminator" technologies, pose substantial risks to agricultural biodiversity and would impart unfavorable characteristics in the crop.

3.6 Pharmacogenomics:-

Scientists do not expect they will discover a single gene for each disease. As a result, they are researching gene interactions and probing populations for differences in the genetic code known as single nucleotide polymorphisms, or SNPs, which may raise one's likelihood of developing a specific disease or determining one's response to a treatment. This remarkable ability to ascribe risk and response to genetic variants is driving the push for "individualized medicine." The goal is to prevent, diagnose, and treat patients more effectively by prescribing interventions based on their genetic traits.

4. Opportunities:-

4.1 Omics biology:-

Omics is a medical profession that investigates biological processes and disorders by observing the aggregate behavior of molecules such as genes, proteins, and metabolites. Its goal is to better understand the molecular foundation of health and disease, which will lead to the creation of novel diagnostic tools and personalized medical techniques. Omics technologies are increasingly being employed in digital health to improve health evaluations, diagnosis, and treatments, including personalized medicine and predictive analytics. Clinical Decision Support Integrating omics data into clinical decision support systems can provide real-time information and recommendations to healthcare practitioners to improve treatment decisions for patients.Omics data collection medical devices Continuous glucose monitoring systems and other medical devices can capture omics data to monitor a patient's health and detect potential difficulties early on integrating omics data into telemedicine systems can improve access to healthcare services and outcomes for those in remote or underprivileged locations, including virtual consultations.

4.2 Developments in medical devices:-

Wearable technology, such as smartwatches and fitness trackers, is growing popularity because of its capacity to track health metrics such as heart rate, sleep patterns, and physical activity. The global market for wearable medical devices is estimated to increase from $22.44 billion in 2022 to $27.37 billion in 2023, with an annual growth rate of 21.9%. Recent ideas include combining augmented reality (AR) technology into wearable devices to improve user experiences and using artificial intelligence (AI) for advanced functionality.

Diagnostic tools, such as glucose meters and spirometry, are critical for diagnosing a variety of illnesses. Point-of-care (POC) devices are widely used for speedy testing in a variety of contexts, whilst non-invasive technologies, such as breath analysis and skin sensors, give a comfortable and simple testing experience, removing the need for invasive procedures such as blood tests.

Wearable therapeutics, non-invasive stimulators, and regenerative therapies are all developing treatment trends. Wearable technologies enable ongoing, non-invasive treatment, such as electrical stimulation for depression or medications for injuries. Non-invasive stimulators use magnetic or electrical fields to stimulate specific brain regions, offering a safe alternative to conventional treatments. Regenerative therapies, such as growth factors delivered to injury sites, promote the growth and regeneration of damaged tissue.

4.3 Nanosensors:-

Food quality monitoring is critical for preventing spoiling and maintaining food integrity. Researchers worldwide have created nanosensors that can detect food pathogens and rotting kinds, paving the way for the development of smart packaging. These sensors identify toxins, monitor food and packaging factors such as time, temperature, and expiration date, and ensure that consumers receive fresh, quality food. They are very beneficial in food packaging and transportation for preserving food quality and safety.

5. Future of the Technology:-

Many people would welcome biotechnology products if they were both beneficial and safe. People are eager to buy pesticide- and insecticide-free crops. People are increasingly accepting vegetables grown without the use of chemical fertilizers or pesticides, which have good nutritional value.The labeling of the product is also an ethical problem, as some argue that marking any product as a biotechnology product may be interpreted as a warning sign by consumers; yet, others believe that labeling should be done since consumers have the right to know what they are eating . The products may be acceptable if customers can accept the food developed from biotechnology after balancing all pros and disadvantages, and if the price is right, has greater nutritional values, is nice in flavor, and is safe to ingest.

Biotechnology is at a crossroads in terms of public anxiety and acceptance. Surprisingly, all medicinal goods are accepted and play an important role in the biopharmaceutical business, while food crops continue to face challenges in terms of global acceptance. The future of global food supply is dependent on how well scientists, governments, and the food business communicate with people about the technology's benefits and safety. Several important attempts are underway to enhance the regulatory process and communicate more effectively with consumers through educational programs. The future of biotechnology seems very promising, and we are excited to be a part of the transmission of these crucial new breakthroughs.

Refrences:-

1. Prajapat R, Jain S. D S A D D A S D MEDICAL REVIEWS Narrative Review Advancement in Medical Biotechnology: A Review. Published online 2022. doi:10.30491/IJMR.2021.279672.1197

2. Chazhaev M. Economic potential of biotechnologies: challenges and windows of opportunity. In: *BIO Web of Conferences*. Vol 76. EDP Sciences; 2023. doi:10.1051/bioconf/20237610002

3. Singh RS, Singh RS. *Industrial Biotechnology: An Overview Chapter 1.* https://www.researchgate.net/publication/311576484

CHAPTER TWELVE

HORIZONS UNVEILED: EMERGING TRENDS AND FUTURE DIRECTIONS IN BIOTECHNOLOGY

INTRODUCTION

The chapter "Horizons Unveiled: Emerging Trends and Future Directions in Biotechnology" invites us to investigate the boundaries of science that are constantly growing. We are at the beginning of a new era where biotechnology is being driven into uncharted terrain by the speed at which technology is developing and the coming together of several fields.

This chapter takes us on a journey of expectation and prediction, guiding us through the innovative currents that will influence biotechnology in the future. Biotechnology is a field that has limitless potential and the ability to revolutionise society, from manipulating genetic code to using artificial intelligence. Our trip delves into the fields of synthetic biology, personalised medicine, and sustainable solutions, pushing the boundaries of conventional wisdom. Here, we see the birth of new approaches, procedures, and paradigms that have the potential to completely alter the definition of what is feasible.

The history of biotechnology is a millennium-long tale of invention, exploration, and change. The history of human civilization has been significantly shaped by biotechnology, from the first agricultural techniques to the most advanced modern technologies.

The history of biotechnology begins in prehistoric societies, when people first discovered how to use living things for constructive reasons. The production of food, drinks, and medications by fermentation—possibly one of the earliest microbiological processes ever discovered by humans—provided the groundwork for the advancement of contemporary biotechnology.

The field of biotechnology is undergoing a significant transition as we approach a new era, propelled by innovative discoveries and advancements in technology. With the ability to manipulate DNA and incorporate state-of-the-art computational techniques, biotechnology presents us with an endless horizon full of unexplored possibilities.

Looking out into the distance, we see possibilities as well as obstacles that need our focus and creativity. As we navigate the uncharted waters of biotechnological innovation, ethical considerations, legal frameworks, and societal repercussions highlight the need for responsible stewardship. Come along as we look towards the future and the promise of a brand-new era in biotechnology. Together, let's explore the new patterns and avenues that will define this amazing field's future and lead us closer to a time when science fiction will become reality and the only boundaries on what can be imagined are our own.

INTRODUCTION TO BIOTECHNOLOGY'S EVOLUTION

The history of biotechnology is a millennium-long tale of invention, exploration, and change. The history of human civilization has been significantly shaped by biotechnology, from the first agricultural techniques to the most advanced modern technologies. The history of biotechnology begins in prehistoric societies, when people first discovered how to use living things for constructive reasons. The production of food, drinks, and medications by fermentation—possibly one of the earliest microbiological processes ever discovered by humans—provided the groundwork for the advancement of contemporary biotechnology.

As scientists started to solve the riddles of microscopic life, the development of microbiology in the 17th century was a turning point in the history of biotechnology. The contributions of Robert Koch, Louis Pasteur, and Antonie van Leeuwenhoek cleared the path for a better comprehension of microbial physiology and the function of microbes in fermentation processes. Thanks to developments in genetics, recombinant DNA technology, and molecular biology, biotechnological innovation grew exponentially in the 20th century. With the ground breaking discovery of DNA's double helix structure by Watson and Crick in 1953, genetic engineering entered a new phase and scientists could now precisely modify genes and engineer entire creatures.

Biotechnology was revolutionised in the 1970s when recombinant DNA technology emerged, enabling scientists to splice and reassemble DNA from many sources to produce unique genetic constructions. This discovery ushered in a new era of biotechnological innovation by laying the foundation for the creation of recombinant proteins, gene treatments, and genetically modified organisms (GMOs). Synthetic biology, systems biology, and bioinformatics are just a few of the new areas that biotechnology has embraced in recent decades. Through the use of these interdisciplinary methodologies, biotechnology has advanced beyond conventional limitations, allowing scientists to precisely and intricately engineer biological systems.

Currently leading the way in scientific research and technological innovation, biotechnology is advancing environmental sustainability, industry, agriculture, medicine, and other fields. The invention of mRNA vaccines and other gene editing technologies like CRISPR-Cas9 are two examples of how biotechnology is changing how we identify, treat, and prevent diseases. The potential is endless as we begin the next phase of biotechnology's development. We get closer to realising biotechnology's full potential to solve some of the most important problems facing humanity and open up new vistas for scientific research with every new discovery and technical advancement.

TRENDS IN SYNTHETIC BIOLOGY

Using concepts from computer science, engineering, and biology, synthetic biology is a cutting-edge field that creates and builds unique biological systems with specific functions. Synthetic biology has seen a number of trends in recent years that have spurred innovation and pushed the envelope of what is possible:

1. Advanced Gene Editing Technologies:

By making it possible to precisely and effectively manipulate DNA sequences, the introduction of sophisticated gene editing tools, including CRISPR-Cas9, has completely changed synthetic biology. With the use of these technologies, scientists can now precisely alter DNA, creating new avenues for creating organisms with the required characteristics.

2. Genome Engineering and Design:

Whole-genome engineering and design, in which entire genomes are synthesised or edited to create creatures with customised features, is a trend in synthetic biology. Applications such as environmental remediation and industrial biomanufacturing could benefit from this strategy.

3. Bioproduction through Metabolic Engineering:

A key component of synthetic biology, metabolic engineering allows for the optimisation of cellular metabolism to produce useful chemicals. Designing and optimising metabolic pathways to increase the yields, titers, and productivities of bioproducts—such as specialised chemicals, biofuels, and pharmaceuticals—has been a popular recent trend.

4. Cell-Free Synthetic Biology:

The field of cell-free synthetic biology is a recent development that uses artificial biomolecular systems or cell extracts to carry out biochemical activities in place of living cells. Benefits from this strategy include improved control over reaction conditions, streamlined genetic circuits, and quick prototyping—all of which open up new possibilities for biomanufacturing, biosensing, and drug discovery.

5. Automation and Standardisation:

To increase repeatability and expedite the design-build-test cycle, automation and standardisation are becoming more and more crucial in synthetic biology. The creation of genetic circuits, automated DNA assembly platforms, and standardised biological components is hastening innovation and facilitating the quick prototyping of artificial biological systems.

6. Synthetic Genomics and DNA Synthesis:

The development of huge DNA structures or complete genomes with precise control over sequence composition is made possible by technological advancements in DNA synthesis, which are propelling advances in synthetic genomics. Applications such as genome writing, genome-scale engineering, and synthetic organism design seem to benefit from this trend.

7. Computational Tools and Design Algorithms:

The logical design and optimisation of synthetic biological systems depend on computational tools and design algorithms. Predictive modelling techniques, machine learning algorithms, and software platforms for modelling and forecasting the behaviour of artificial biological systems are among the trends in this field.

PERSONALIZED MEDICINE AND PRECISION BIOTECHNOLOGY

A paradigm shift in healthcare is being brought about by precision biotechnology and personalised medicine, which seek to customise medical procedures and therapies to the unique needs of each patient. These methods make use of developments in targeted medicines, genomics, and molecular diagnostics to provide more accurate, focused, and individualised healthcare.

1. Genomic Medicine:

This refers to the application of genomic data, including genetic mutations and variations, to inform medical choices and treatment plans. With the development of genome-wide association studies (GWAS) and high-throughput sequencing technology, scientists are now able to pinpoint the genetic causes of diseases and create personalised treatments based on a person's genetic profile.

2. Finding and validating biomarkers:

Biological signs that can forecast disease risk, course, and response to therapy—is essential to precision biotechnology. The goal of biomarker discovery initiatives is to find biological signatures linked to certain diseases or treatment outcomes using genomics, proteomics, metabolomics, and other omics technologies.

3. Targeted Therapies:

With precision biotechnology, disease-causing genes, proteins, or pathways can be specifically targeted with minimal adverse effects on healthy tissues. This strategy makes use of gene therapies, RNA-based treatments, monoclonal antibodies, and molecularly targeted medications that aim to disrupt particular molecular targets linked to the aetiology of disease.

4. Pharmacogenomics:

The goal of pharmacogenomics is to maximise medicine choice, dosage, and effectiveness for every patient by investigating the connection between genetic differences and unique pharmacological reactions. Healthcare professionals can anticipate medication responses, spot possible side effects, and tailor treatment plans to optimise therapeutic results by examining a patient's genetic composition.

5. Companion Diagnostics:

Molecular tests known as companion diagnostics are used to determine which individuals are most likely to benefit from a specific therapeutic intervention. In order to stratify patients based on biomarker expression levels, genetic mutations, or other molecular traits and make sure that treatments are given to individuals who are most likely to respond favourably, these tests are frequently developed in conjunction with targeted medications.

6. Digital Health Technologies:

Wearable sensors, mobile health applications, and remote monitoring devices are examples of digital health technologies that are included in precision biotechnology. These technologies allow for real-time data analysis and continuous monitoring of patient health parameters. In order to improve patient outcomes, these technologies provide early intervention techniques, remote patient monitoring, and personalised illness treatment.

7. Ethical and Regulatory Considerations:

The use of precision biotechnology and personalised medicine brings up significant ethical, legal, and societal issues pertaining to data security, privacy, consent, and fair access to healthcare. In order to protect patient rights, advance accountability and transparency, and enable the responsible development, validation, and application of new technologies, regulatory frameworks must change.

DIGITAL BIOTECHNOLOGY AND DATA-DRIVEN INSIGHTS

In order to better understand, predict, and manage biological processes, digital biotechnology combines biotechnology with digital technologies including big data analytics, artificial intelligence (AI), and machine learning (ML). This multidisciplinary strategy has the power to transform healthcare, speed up scientific research, and improve bioprocesses.

1. Big Data Analytics:

The analysis of vast amounts of biological data produced by sources like proteomics, metabolomics, and genomics using sophisticated computer methods is known as big data analytics. Through the extraction of significant insights from intricate datasets, big data analytics helps researchers find trends, correlations, and patterns that would be missed by more conventional analytical techniques.

2. Artificial Intelligence (AI):

To process and analyse biological data, artificial intelligence includes machine learning algorithms and cognitive computing systems that imitate human intellect. AI systems in the field of biotechnology are capable of learning to identify patterns in biological data, forecast results, and direct judgement calls in fields like illness diagnosis, drug development, and biomarker identification.

3. Machine Learning (ML):

Without explicit programming, machine learning methods allow computers to learn from data and gradually improve their performance. ML techniques are applied in biotechnology to predict biological features, model intricate biological systems, and optimise experimental designs, resulting in more effective drug development, metabolic engineering, and personalised medicine methods.

4. Predictive modelling:

It is the process of creating simulations and mathematical models to forecast how biological systems will behave in certain scenarios. Predictive models can simulate biochemical reactions, cellular functions, and organismal behaviour by fusing biological knowledge with computing methods. This helps with the design and optimisation of biotechnological processes and products.

5. Precision Medicine and Healthcare:

Precision medicine is the application of patient-specific data analysis, such as genomic information, electronic health records, and wearable sensor data, to customise medical interventions and treatments for individual patients. This is made possible by digital biotechnology. Digital biotechnology's data-driven insights enable healthcare professionals to make well-informed decisions, optimise treatment plans, and enhance patient outcomes.

6. Bioprocess Optimization:

Digital biotechnology is a key component of industrial biotechnology when it comes to optimising bioprocesses for the generation of biopharmaceuticals, biofuels, and other bioproducts. Digital biotechnology allows for the optimisation of fermentation conditions, metabolic pathways, and downstream processing procedures, resulting in higher productivity, efficiency, and product quality. This is achieved by combining real-time monitoring, sensor data, and predictive modelling.

7. Possibilities and Challenges:

The implementation of digital biotechnology brings with it potential as well as difficulties with data integration, privacy issues, computational infrastructure, and workforce development. To overcome these obstacles, biologists, computer scientists, engineers, and legislators must work together to create strong data management plans, moral standards, and legal frameworks that guarantee the ethical application of digital technologies in biotechnology.

SUSTAINABILITY AND GREEN BIOTECHNOLOGY

1. Renewable Resources:

The main goal of green biotechnology is to employ renewable resources as feedstocks for bioprocesses, such as algae, plant biomass, and agricultural waste. Green biotechnology lessens environmental effect and decreases dependency on finite fossil fuels by employing renewable resources.

2. Bio-Based Materials:

Green biotechnology makes it possible to produce bio-based materials from renewable feedstocks, including biodegradable polymers, biofuels, and biomaterials. These materials aid in the shift to a circular economy by providing environmentally friendly substitutes for traditional petroleum-based products.

3. Bioremediation:

Bioremediation is the process of removing or breaking down pollutants and toxins from the environment by using living organisms like fungi, bacteria, and plants. Green biotechnology provides environmentally acceptable ways to purify tainted air, water, and soil, helping to mitigate pollution and rebuild ecosystems.

4. Carbon Capture and Utilisation (CCU):

Utilising photosynthetic organisms like cyanobacteria and microalgae, green biotechnology helps sequester carbon dioxide from industrial emissions and transform it into useful products like food additives, chemicals, and biofuels.

5. Sustainable Agriculture:

By creating crop types with increased production, disease resistance, and environmental tolerance, green biotechnology supports sustainable agriculture methods. Green biotechnology increases agricultural output while reducing inputs and environmental effect through genetic engineering, precision breeding, and microbiome engineering.

6. Waste Valorization:

Organic waste streams, including food waste, agricultural leftovers, and municipal solid waste, can be valued and turned into products with additional value, such biofuels, bioplastics, and biochemicals, thanks to green biotechnology. Green biotechnology decreases landfilling and incineration and increases resource efficiency by turning waste into resources.

7. Biodiversity Conservation:

By maintaining and rehabilitating natural habitats, safeguarding endangered species, and encouraging sustainable land management techniques, green biotechnology contributes to biodiversity conservation initiatives. Green biotechnology supports ecological balance and environmental sustainability by boosting biodiversity and ecosystem resilience.

8. Policy and Regulation:

Frameworks that support social responsibility, environmental preservation, and sustainability have an impact on the uptake of green biotechnology. Governments, business associations, and non-governmental groups work together to create guidelines and regulations that facilitate the ethical application of biotechnology for sustainable development.

BIOPHARMACEUTICAL INNOVATIONS

1. Gene therapies:

To treat genetic abnormalities, malignancies, and other diseases, therapeutic genes are delivered to specific cells or tissues. Developments in viral vectors, delivery methods, and gene editing technologies are broadening the application and effectiveness of gene therapy techniques, potentially providing treatments for diseases that were previously incurable.

2. Cell-Based Therapies:

Utilising cells' immunomodulatory and regenerative abilities, cell-based therapies aim to heal wounds and illnesses. This covers treatments like CAR-T cell therapy for cancer, tissue engineering methods for regenerative medicine, and stem cell transplants. Next-generation cell therapies are being developed as a result of advancements in genetic engineering, cell delivery strategies, and cell culture techniques.

3. RNA Therapeutics:

Small interfering RNA (siRNA), microRNA (miRNA), and antisense oligonucleotides are examples of the large class of nucleic acid-based medications known as RNA therapies. These compounds provide prospective therapies for genetic abnormalities, viral infections, and neurological diseases by targeting RNA molecules involved in disease processes.

4. Biobetters and Biosimilars:

Biobetters are the next generation of biopharmaceuticals that aim to enhance the efficacy, safety, or patient convenience of current biologics. Biosimilars are very similar copies of currently available biologics that provide affordable substitutes for name-brand biopharmaceuticals. The creation of biobetters and biosimilars is being propelled by advancements in protein engineering, formulation technologies, and manufacturing procedures.

5. Drug Delivery Systems:

Biopharmaceuticals' pharmacokinetics, biodistribution, and therapeutic efficacy are all greatly enhanced by effective drug delivery systems. Improvements in targeted drug delivery strategies, hydrogels, liposomes, and nanoparticle-based delivery systems are enhancing the release and transport of biologics, leading to better therapeutic results and fewer adverse effects.

6. Personalised Medicine Techniques:

Techniques use genomic, proteomic, and other omics data to customise medical therapies based on the unique genetic composition, illness profiles, and response to therapy of each patient. These methods make precision medicine techniques possible, including as patient stratification for targeted medicines, companion diagnostics, and medication therapy guided by pharmacogenomics.

ETHICAL, LEGAL, AND SOCIETAL IMPLICATIONS

1. Privacy and Data Security:

Ethical issues related to the gathering, archiving, and distribution of genetic and biological data.
safeguarding people's confidentiality and privacy in the big data and genomic sequencing era.

2. Informed Consent and Autonomy:

The significance of informed consent in biotechnological research and medical interventions is highlighted by the concept of autonomy. Honouring people's autonomy and freedom to make knowledgeable decisions about taking part in medical research and receiving treatment.

3. Fair Biotechnological Innovation Access:

Reducing inequalities in biotechnological innovation availability due to socioeconomic position, location, or other variables. ensuring that everyone in society has affordable and easy access to biotechnological advancements.

4. Intellectual property rights:

Moral and legal issues related to biotechnological invention patenting and commercialization.
striking a balance between the need to reward innovation and the advancement of science and public health.

5. Regulatory Governance and Oversight:

The function of regulatory bodies in directing the creation, examination, and marketing of biotechnological goods.Ensuring that legal frameworks are strong, open, and flexible enough to change quickly with the biotechnology industry.

6. Bifunctionality and Biosafety Concerns:

Moral conundrums brought on by biotechnology research's dual-use potential, which could be applied to both good and bad ends. Techniques for encouraging ethical behaviour and reducing the dangers of biological warfare, bioterrorism, and unintentional discharge of dangerous substances.

7. Professional Ethics and Conduct:

The observance of ethical norms and professional behaviour in the field of biotechnology research, development, and application. Promoting a climate of honesty, openness, and responsibility among scientists, engineers, medical experts, and business partners.

8. Social responsibility and Public Participation:

Promoting public involvement and active participation in conversations regarding the moral, legal, and societal ramifications of biotechnology. Encouraging responsiveness, inclusivity, and openness in the processes used to make decisions about biotechnology advancements and regulations.

FUTURE PROSPECTS

1. Convergence of Technologies:

Biotechnology, nanotechnology, artificial intelligence (AI), and robotics are among the technologies that are expected to converge in the future and shape the field of biotechnology. When these domains are integrated, highly complex and multipurpose biotechnological systems with a range of uses in industry, healthcare, agriculture, and environmental sustainability may be developed.

2. Biomimicry and Bioinspiration:

It is anticipated that biological systems and the design principles found in nature will serve as sources of inspiration for future biotechnological advancements. Biomimetic techniques, which imitate the composition and capabilities of natural materials and animals, may result in the creation of novel biomaterials, robots with bioinspired designs, and bioengineered solutions to difficult problems.

3. Synthetic Biology 2.0:

Synthetic Biology 2.0 is the next stage of synthetic biology that is expected to further push the limits of biological design and genetic engineering. This might entail the synthesis of minimum genomes, synthetic cells, and protocells in addition to the production of artificial ecosystems and programmable organisms with hitherto unheard-of powers.

4. Bioinformatics and Biological Computing:

Developments in these fields are predicted to completely transform data processing, computation, and storage utilising biological systems and molecules. Biologically inspired algorithms, molecular computing, and DNA-based storage may open up new possibilities for machine learning, parallel processing, and high-density data storage.

5. Environmental Biotechnology:

In order to address global issues including pollution, resource depletion, and climate change, biotechnological solutions for environmental sustainability are anticipated to be vital. Prospects for the future include bio-based fuel substitutes, bioremediation technology for removing contaminants from contaminated areas, and biologically inspired methods for waste management and sustainable agriculture.

6. Environmental Biotechnology:

In order to address global issues including pollution, resource depletion, and climate change, biotechnological solutions for environmental sustainability are anticipated to be vital. Prospects for the future include bio-based fuel substitutes, bioremediation technology for removing contaminants from contaminated areas, and biologically inspired methods for waste management and sustainable agriculture.

REFERENCE

1. National Academies of Sciences, Engineering, and Medicine. (2017). Biotechnology Research in an Age of Terrorism. National Academies Press.

2. Biotechnology Innovation Organization. (2020). The State of Innovation in Highly Prevalent Chronic Diseases: Genomics, Big Data, and Artificial Intelligence. Retrieved from https://www.bio.org/sites/default/files/policy/2019/2019-BIO-Global-Biotech-Report.pdf

3. World Health Organization. (2021). Global Observatory on Health R&D. Retrieved from https://www.who.int/research-observatory/monitoring/inputs/biotechnology/en/

4. European Commission. (2020). Biotechnology Report. Retrieved from https://ec.europa.eu/growth/sectors/biotechnology_en

5. National Institutes of Health. (2020). Biotechnology and Bioengineering Research. Retrieved from https://www.nih.gov/science/biotechnology-

bioengineering

6. United Nations Industrial Development Organization. (2019). Biotechnology for Sustainable Industrial Development. Retrieved from https://www.unido.org/themes/biotechnology-sustainable-industrial-development

7. Royal Society. (2021). Future Biotechnologies: Towards Sustainable Development. Retrieved from https://royalsociety.org/topics-policy/projects/future-biotechnologies/

8. Biotechnology Industry Organization. (2020). Biotechnology: Unlocking the Potential of Nature. Retrieved from https://www.bio.org/policy/biotechnology-unlocking-potential-nature

9. World Economic Forum. (2020). Biotechnology Innovation Landscape. Retrieved from https://www.weforum.org/reports/biotechnology-innovation-landscape

10. National Science Foundation. (2021). Biotechnology and Biological Sciences. Retrieved from https://www.nsf.gov/div/index.jsp?div=BIO

Afterword

DEAR READERS,

As we reach the culmination of our journey through "Biotech Horizon," we are filled with gratitude for the opportunity to explore the vast landscape of biotechnology with you. In these fourteen chapters, we embarked on a voyage of discovery, delving into the frontiers of science and the ethical considerations that accompany the remarkable advancements in this field.

From the intricacies of genetic engineering to the promise of personalized medicine, each chapter sought to illuminate both the awe-inspiring potential and the complex implications of biotechnology. We witnessed how biotech is revolutionizing agriculture, healthcare, and industry, offering solutions to some of the most pressing challenges facing humanity.

Yet, as we marveled at the possibilities, we also confronted the ethical dilemmas inherent in wielding such transformative power. Questions of equity, accessibility, and the unintended consequences of genetic manipulation loomed large, reminding us of the importance of thoughtful reflection and responsible stewardship in our pursuit of progress.

As we bid farewell to these pages, let us carry forward the lessons learned and the conversations sparked by our exploration of "Biotech Horizon." May we continue to engage with curiosity and compassion, ever mindful of the potential for both innovation and impact in the realm of biotechnology.

Thank you for joining us on this journey. The horizon beckons, and the future awaits our careful and considered embrace.

Warm regards,

Dr. Rajesh Jorgewad

Dhanwantari Desai

Abhishek Mohite

Aditya Pillai